The Haydens: Nicky, Tommy, & Roger

The Haydens: Nicky, Tommy, & Roger
From OWB to MotoGP

Chris Jonnum

FOREWORD BY GARY NIXON

DESIGN BY TOM MORGAN

DAVID BULL PUBLISHING

Chris Jonnum and the Hayden family dedicate this book to the memory of Ethan Gillim.

Library of Congress Control Number: 200792961

ISBN-13: 978 1 893618 81 7

ISBN-10: 1 893618 81 1

David Bull Publishing, logo, and colophon are trademarks of David Bull Publishing, Inc.

Book and cover design: Tom Morgan, Blue Design, Portland, Maine

Printed in Hong Kong

10 9 8 7 6 5 4 3 2 1

David Bull Publishing
4250 East Camelback Road
Suite K150
Phoenix, AZ 85018
602-852-9500
602-852-9503 (fax)

www.bullpublishing.com

PAGE 2: With his likeness watching over him, Nicky Hayden heads to his second Red Bull USGP victory at Mazda Raceway Laguna Seca, in 2006. At that season's final round, he would wrap up the MotoGP world championship. (Andrew Northcott)

RIGHT: At a winter test between the 2004 and 2005 seasons, Roger interviews his big brother in the Kawasaki semi for a *Road Racer X* magazine story on Tommy's first AMA Supersport championship title. (Riles/Nelson)

PAGE 6: Tommy at speed on his Kawasaki ZX-6R in AMA Supersport competition in 2002. (Riles/Nelson)

PAGE 7: Nicky, Tommy, and Roger enjoy the moment together on the MotoGP grid at the Valencia, Spain round in 2004. This was Nicky's first season in MotoGP (Andrew Northcott).

CONTENTS

Foreword

by Gary Nixon

I've been running with the Hayden family since before the kids were even born, but the only problem was I didn't know them at the time! Earl and I used to do the same act in the '60s—racing on the same Midwestern short tracks—but we just never ran into each other back then. I went on to get my AMA Grand National Championships in 1967 and '68, and although Earl never really made it as a successful racer, he certainly has shown that he knows how to raise them.

I met "Fast" Eddie Thompson, the Hayden kids' cousin, at a couple of races, but I didn't actually get to know the Haydens until Jim France sponsored the Super Team Yamaha effort at Daytona in 1985. I was the manager, and our A team had Jay Springsteen, Jimmy Filice, Steve Parrish, and Lance Jones. Lance was hanging around with the Haydens back then, and the kids came walking up to the pits to check everything out.

I remember noticing how cute those little kids were, and I liked them a lot right away. Tommy, Jenny, and Nicky had a little minibike, and they were so interested in all the famous riders and the race bikes. Roger was barely walking at the time, and I think Rose was still pregnant with Kathleen.

I've been friends with the Haydens ever since, but it wasn't like I took them under my wing and showed them the ropes. Basically, I just consider myself lucky enough to have gotten to hang out with them, but one thing I did tell them was to keep it on the straight and narrow, which probably sounded kind of funny coming from me. I was definitely pretty rough around the edges when I was racing—hey, it was the '60s and '70s, after all—and I hung out with the wrong people when I had

some injuries, which didn't help my career much. The Hayden kids have always been pretty straight arrows, though. They've avoided all the traps that get so many promising racers, and they even go to church.

Even back when they were kids, the boys all had such different personalities. Tommy was quiet and would always keep about a percent in reserve—he very seldom crashes—whereas Nicky would just put it all on the line. One of my strongest memories of Nicky is in the Half-Mile at the 1996 Amateur Nationals in Indianapolis. It was one of the most incredible last laps I've ever seen, with Nicky completely sideways out on the cushion—inches away from a concrete wall with no hay bales—holding it wide-open to try and get around another kid.

I actually asked for his autograph after that, and it must have been one of his first ones, because you can actually read it!

Back then, Roger was just a chubby little kid coming up, but I knew he was paying attention: At that same Amateur Nationals race, I noticed him sitting up when he was coming down the straightaway. I told Earl he needed to tell Rog to start tucking in, and I don't think I've seen a photo of him since where he wasn't completely tucked!

Each of the kids has always had a kind of role, and I think that as the oldest brother, Tommy's has been to kind of check things out for his brothers. When he started racing dirt track as a pro, people didn't really know who he was, but he was studying everything, learning a lot, and passing it down. Then when Nicky came along, he benefited from Tommy's trailblazing and took it up to the next level. Nicky also has that great, outgoing personality and smile (I still can't believe they haven't gotten him an endorsement deal with a toothpaste company!), and he was blessed with a lot of self-confidence. I can honestly say that Nicky is the best rider I've ever seen come up through the

ranks. Granted, I wasn't over in Italy when Valentino Rossi was a kid, but as far as I'm concerned, there's no doubt that Nicky is one of the best riders in the world. The fact that he's got a personality to go along with it is just a bonus.

Whereas Nicky always caught on right away, it took Roger a little longer. Part of that is because the bikes were junk by the time they were handed down to him, but I think he was also processing the information he was getting from seeing both of his older brothers in action. I really do think he still has huge potential. And let's not forget that Jenny beat them all a few times!

One of the things I like most about the Haydens is that they came up through dirt track, just like we old guys did. Whereas it was injuries that forced me to switch to road racing full-time, the Haydens did it because they were smart enough to see that the racing world was changing, and that this is where the future was. I think their dirt track backgrounds help them to control their bikes. I've seen photos of Nicky with his Repsol Honda sideways, and that just comes from drafting Springer off of turn

four at Springfield. I guess the new thing in MotoGP is to ride with your wheels in line, but I still think that knowing how to dirt track is handy when things get out of shape.

Maybe just as important, coming up through dirt track gave the Haydens a respect for motorcycle racing's history, which is appropriate since they ended up making some history of their own. When they switched over to road racing, I told Earl that they would eventually sweep a podium in that sport, but it was nice that when they did end up doing it, it was back in dirt track—at the 2002 Springfield TT.

I thought their real success would come in road racing though, and I was right. Nicky became world champion, he and Tommy both won titles in AMA racing, and I'm sure Roger will get his soon. Back in 1976, international politics cost me the Formula 750 title—and the opportunity to be America's first world champion—so it was really gratifying to see Nicky get the MotoGP crown in 2006. I was lucky enough to be there in Valencia when he wrapped it up, and I watched those final laps on a giant screen beside the track as I sat on a scooter with my buddy, Charles Herron, in turn one. I've been pulling for the Haydens for so long that it was almost as good as if I had gotten the championship myself!

I still follow the Haydens' careers very closely, whether it be watching an AMA race on television or hitting a couple of MotoGP rounds every season. I always wear Nicky's No. 69 hat when I'm overseas, and I've had people come up and congratulate me on how great my sons are and ask me for an autograph. Considering that I got two Grand National Championships, while Earl backed out of racing to focus on raising his kids, it's kind of funny that *I'm* the one being mistaken for *him*!

How could a kid ask for a better mom and dad than Rose and Earl? I know Earl wasn't always an angel, but having kids inspired him to straighten up. Ever since I've known them, it has been obvious that their kids are the most important thing

in the world to them. Earl decided early on that these kids were going to be successful racers, but he didn't just pay their way through like some other parents have done. Granted, it wasn't cheap to load up the van and drive off to different races every weekend—what money they did have, they spent on racing—but they didn't always have the best equipment. It really has paid off, but honestly, I think something that was at least as big a factor in their success was Earl's salesmanship. He was so good at talking to people and creating opportunities for his kids, and just as important, he was a very likable guy.

Partly because of that, so many people have played parts in the Haydens' careers, whether it was sponsors, team owners, other racers, mechanics, or just people putting in a good word for them. It seemed like folks just saw something special in the Hayden family, and they wanted to be a small part of the success that they felt sure the kids were destined to enjoy.

That's one reason I'm so excited about this book. A lot of those people who helped the Haydens are mentioned in here, which is nice for them, but it's even better for all the people who *weren't* involved. The Hayden family really does have an incredible story; I got to see it, and I'm glad that so many other people are going to finally get the chance to read it.

CHAPTER 1

PODIUM SWEEP

FAR LEFT: Nicky puts down his steel-shoe-clad left foot and pitches his CRF450R sideways in a Springfield corner. The bike was perfectly suited for the track conditions, and Nicky put it to good use. (Flat Trak Fotos)
MIDDLE: Roger and Nicky spray Earl with champagne in the winner's circle. In Owensboro the previous week, Earl had built a practice track that emulated the Springfield TT circuit. "By the time we got to Springfield, I bet we had made 10,000 laps on that practice track," Earl says. (Flat Trak Fotos)
RIGHT: Mechanic Dan Fahie gets the honor of a victory-lap ride with Nicky and the checkered flag. The mechanic has been a big part of all three Hayden brothers' careers over the years. (Flat Trak Fotos)

ABOVE: The front row for the main event, with Roger (34), Chris Carr (1), Tommy (22), and Nicky (69) eagerly awaiting the start. "When my dad told me I got pole, I thought he was kidding me," Roger says, "but he said, 'You know I wouldn't kid you about something like that.'" (Flat Trak Fotos)
OPPOSITE: The Springfield crowd cuts loose with Nicky after the race. "Everybody was excited that the Haydens were there in the first place," says the IMDA's executive director, Tommra Luparell, "but I don't think anybody actually thought that they'd sweep the whole thing." (Flat Trak Fotos)

With one final flip of the tire lever, Dan Fahie popped the Goodyear bead onto the rim and stood up straight to stretch his back. The soft dirt track tires are hell to install, and over the course of the past few days, Fahie had repeated the process countless times. Although he was the chassis mechanic for Nicky Hayden's factory Honda superbike road racer during the 2002 season, this dirt track stuff was pretty foreign to him; with the marathon schedule and the Hayden brothers constantly asking his advice, however, he was definitely getting up to speed.

"Pass me that air hose, will you, Tommy?" Fahie called out to Nicky's older brother, who was standing at a workbench, working a fresh air filter onto its cage. Over in a corner, the youngest Hayden brother, Roger Lee, was draining a bike's engine oil into a pan. As Dan began airing up the tire, he could see through the open garage door that Nicky was taking advantage of the last minutes of daylight, spraying down his practice bike with a pressure washer in the driveway.

The occasion for all the activity was tomorrow's Springfield TT— a classic dirt track event held at the end of May—which the Hayden brothers had decided to enter. The history books had no record of three brothers ever having qualified for the same final in an AMA National Championship event, but the Haydens figured they had a chance. All three were now full-time professional road racers, but the prospect of making history had called them back to their dirt track roots for this one weekend. Honda also realized the potential of the moment, and they'd not only endorsed Nicky's participation, but also shipped him a special race bike and sent Fahie out to the Haydens' Owensboro, Kentucky, home from American Honda's Southern California headquarters. Tommy and Roger's teams (Kawasaki and Erion Honda, respectively) had also approved their participation in the race, but both were essentially on their own; that meant Fahie was assisting them as well. The past five days had seen the group testing and wrenching until 1:00 a.m., with the only respite coming from a few hours of sleep each night and the periodic clanging of mother Rose's dinner bell.

Fortunately, Fahie and the Haydens had help in the form of a group of longtime buddies: As Fahie rolled the freshly shod wheel over to Nicky's race bike, which was placed on a hydraulic lift in the middle of the gray garage floor, he had to run a slalom between Clint "Sloppy" Simmons, Chris "Digger" Phelps, Chad Burcham, Darrell "Tater Tot" Stallings (all of whom were scattered about the garage, busy with various tasks), and Eric "Reynolds Wrap" Reynolds (who was leaning back in a tattered easy chair, keeping up a steady commentary on the garage's organized chaos). Earl, the Hayden boys' father, had run the stopwatch all week and was now busy preparing the family's race van for the trip.

"Okay, boys, we'd better get things finished and loaded up," Dan announced. "It's a five-hour drive to Springfield, and you guys are going to need some sleep. You've got a big day tomorrow."

Ask average American citizens for their thoughts on Springfield—one of this country's most common city names—and they're likely to mention the animated metropolis that is home to television's cartoon Simpson family. Residents of the Midwest (or those who paid attention in high school geography and history) might remember that it's the capital of Illinois and the longtime residence of President Abraham Lincoln. But to motorcycle aficionados, Springfield means just one thing: dirt track racing.

The majestic Illinois State Fairgrounds, situated on the north end of town, has hosted motorcycle races since the beginning of the 20th century. There are records of Springfield races as far back as 1911, and for a while, the national champion was determined by just the Springfield Mile. After a long hiatus prompted by an overly rowdy crowd, it was revived in 1981 by the Illinois Motorcycle Dealers Association (IMDA, a not-for-profit trade group for the state's motorcycle retailers).

Sanctioned by the American Motorcycle Association (AMA, later to become the American Motorcyc*list* Association), the race was the crown jewel in the Grand National Championship.

When the fairgrounds built a new venue to host the National High School Rodeo in 2000, the IMDA—wanting to round out the race package—began putting on an eighth-mile short track and a TT (a race with jumps and turns in both directions, whereas standard dirt tracks run only counterclockwise on flat ovals). Since then, the Mile has been run twice per year, on Memorial and Labor Day weekends, with the TT National sharing the former date and the Short Track the latter.

When the Hayden clan headed to Springfield for the sophomore running of the TT on May 26, 2002, Tommy, Nicky, and Roger Lee were hoping to add their family name to the venue's rich history. Aged 23, 20, and 18, respectively, the trio knew there was a good chance that they could all qualify for the main event, and some even dared whisper that they might sweep the podium.

AMA Pro Racing has a history of fast brothers—Kenny Roberts Jr. and Kurtis Roberts; Ben and Eric Bostrom; Chuck, Larry, and Denny Palmgren in the '60s and '70s; and Jimmy, Pete, and Steve Chann in the '40s and '50s—but no three brothers in any discipline had ever come close to sweeping the podium. That said, the Haydens had actually done it themselves at the amateur level 11 years earlier. At the AMA Amateur National Dirt Track in Peoria, Illinois, on July 15, 1989, Tommy, Nicky, and sister Jenny had dominated the 65cc TT, taking the top three positions. "At the time, we thought that was just about as good as it could get," father Earl remembers with a laugh.

That Amateur Nationals benchmark wasn't all the Haydens had going in their favor. One year earlier, at the

DATE

ckle funny bones

Here's a sample:

During "Jenny-Wury," readers are advised to grow a beard because "You'll save on neckties." On the "Aperull" page, one finds the following advice: "If yer lookin' fer a helping hand, it's rite there at the end of yer arm," and "nothing increases a golf score like witnesses." By the time "Sip-Tembur" rolls around, one learns that "you can lead a horse to water, but if you teach him to fly, you'd really have something," and the thought for the day — "in just two days tomorrow will be yesterday."

There's a lot more —

See Date/Page 3B

MOTORCYCLE RACING

Roger Hayden hangs on to claim Supersport race

From wire, staff reports

Owensboro's Roger Hayden kept his 2004 Pro Honda Oils Supersport championship hopes alive with his third consecutive win Sunday at Road Atlanta.

Hayden battled throughout the event with his key rival — Kawasaki teammate and brother Tommy Hayden — along with Jason DiSalvo.

Roger opened lap 13 of 15 in third but took the lead on the final lap. Roger, Tommy and DiSalvo ran nose-to-tail along the long back straightaway before swinging into different lanes for a final breaking duel. All three stayed in their lanes and held their positions to the flag.

"The race went pretty good," Roger said. "I never really got worried because if I ever lost a little bit here or there, I could always make it up real quick. When Tommy got the lead, I could tell he going to try to breakaway ... but once again my bike was the fastest one out there. So no matter how far back I was, I could reel him in."

Despite seeing his brother win again, Tommy is in good shape heading into the final round Sept. 17-19 at Virginia International Raceway in Alton, Va. Thanks to claiming the pole and leading the most laps, he only gave up two points to Roger on the weekend and will carry an 11-point advantage (327-316) into the season finale.

"I'll just go into Virginia with an 11-point lead," Tommy said. "I don't need to win, but I'd like to at least get on the podium."

■ Tommy Hayden took third place and Roger Hayden fourth

LOCAL SPORTS

MOTORCYCLE RACING

Nicky Hayden fastest in MotoGP testing

Team travels to Australia for three days of testing

Messenger-Inquirer

Owensboro motorcycle racer Nicky Hayden and Honda Repsol teammate Alex Barros concluded the three-day MotoGP test Friday in Sepang, Malaysia, happy with their work.

Hayden's team packed up at lunch after the 22-year-old set a blistering pace in the morning session. Barros took a long break after lunch after a punishing morning to resume later in the day. He finished 11th.

The team travels to Australia for the scheduled test Tuesday, Wednesday and Thursday at Phillip Island.

Hayden posted the fastest time Friday in the 92-degree heat of 2:01.94 and was pleased with the progress he and the team had made in Sepang.

"I'd be lying if I said it didn't feel good, but I've got to remember this is still only practice," Hayden said. "It really helps to be comfortable with the team, and I think it shows. We've done a good job over the last few days, and I'm happy.

"We've had a few problems, but we are more experienced about fixing them now. I've never been that good in testing — I'm usually best on Sunday so we're feeling positive. The bike feels good. Honda have made a great bike even better over the winter."

MOTORCYCLE RACING

Hayden brothers take 1-2-3 finish

From wire, staff reports

It was history, Hayden style, at round three of the Progressive Insurance U.S. Flat Track Championships.

Owensboro's Nicky, Tommy and Roger Lee Hayden finished 1-2-3 on Saturday at the Springfield TT Dirt Track Race in Springfield, Ill.

Nicky wedged his way by Tommy early and disappeared en route to a comfortable win. Tommy was an easy second, but the big news was Roger Lee holding off the defending Grand National Champion Chris Carr for the last podium spot, making it an unheard of family sweep of the top three positions.

It was obvious all day the Haydens were the class of the field as they swept three of the top four qualifying heats. Roger Lee had the fast heat, putting him on the pole for the main.

Nicky Hayden became the first full-time roadracer to take a break from winning Superbike races to win on the dirt track in several years.

All three brothers rode converted motocross bikes.

Aces: Jessica Velotta top returning

Nicky Hayden update

Owensboro native and MotoGP racer Nicky Hayden flew back to America on Saturday, still recovering from the broken collarbone he suffered last weekend at a training session in Italy.

The 23-year-old took advice from the medical staff who had cared for him since the accident, and the Repsol Honda Team. Hayden hopes to return to action in Japan.

Dapper Don Catti given

Motorsport

Tommy Hayden signs with

small-town kid chased most elusive prize

Roger Lee Hayden signs with Kawasaki

JAMIE ___
No Stories Please!

'There's light at the end of the tunnel. It may not be a beacon, but it's promising.'

Squid

'You better clean up your act'

Photo Gallery

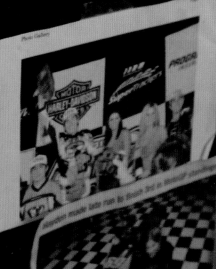

ABOVE: The entire Hayden family (from left) Tommy, Jennifer, Nicky, Rose, Roger Lee, Earl, and Kathleen, pause for a photo during the day program at Springfield. Hours later, the brothers would make history. (Shogo Nakao)

RIGHT: This is the garage in which the Haydens prepared for their assault on the 2002 Springfield TT. It was significantly more crowded during that time! (Chris Jonnum)

Tommy (22) and Chris Carr mix it up during the daytime program. Although some racers resented being shown up by the part-time dirt trackers, most—including Carr—were happy to have the Haydens at Springfield, even if it meant losing to them. "I won the non-Hayden race," Carr jokes. (Flat Trak Fotos)

inaugural Springfield TT, Tommy had scored his first dirt track Grand National win, barely edging out Nicky at the finish. (Roger, after making the main for the first time ever, had placed seventh.) It was an incredible race—the first Grand National dirt track victory by a Yamaha in two decades—and many still talk about it. The year before that, Nicky had won the Springfield Short Track.

In addition, a couple of weeks prior to race day, Earl had taken the exceptional measure of building a track that mimicked the Springfield layout. Under his watchful eye, the brothers had turned countless laps around the replica circuit, with Roger—the least experienced of the three—gaining valuable know-how from his older brothers. Not that they were always on the track together: "Sometimes, we'd get a little too competitive, and Dad would have to make us ride separately," Tommy admits.

Despite the exceptional preparation, there were plenty of obstacles between the Haydens and a Springfield sweep, the most obvious of which was Chris Carr. A previous Grand National Champion (soon to be a multitime champ and later to set a world speed record), Carr had enjoyed such dominant success at the Peoria TT—the AMA national series' other major TT race, where he had won 12 times at that point—that he had earned the nickname Prince of Peoria. Carr wouldn't be easy to beat.

Another obstacle was the Haydens' relative lack of recent professional dirt track experience. Though their roots were in the genre, the brothers had lately been focusing on road racing, and with the responsibilities that come with employment on a major racing team, none had had time to race on a dirt oval that season. Roger, who had never notched a podium finish in a National dirt track, was coming off of a knee injury; and it was the first time Tommy had ridden a flat track in anger since the previous Springfield race.

In fact, the brothers' participation in the race was a

bit of a risk. Nicky was in the hunt for the AMA Superbike Championship, and doing Springfield could potentially jeopardize that important effort. Fortunately, Honda racing manager Chuck Miller gave his blessing and approved having the special bike built. Nicky had flown out to California to test a couple of times with Honda motocross technician Ron Wood at the Corona ranch of Ken Maely, the inventor of the steel shoe that dirt trackers use to help their left foot slide smoothly across the ground. The bike was eventually shipped to the Haydens in Owensboro and was waiting when Fahie arrived. "Nicky really wanted to win," says Fahie. "This was a big deal—a *big* deal."

Kevin Erion—owner of Erion Racing—had also signed off on Roger Lee's participation, and, like Nicky, he'd be on a Honda CRF450R. Big brother, however, was in a rather delicate situation in his first year on the Kawasaki team. At the time, the manufacturer didn't offer a model that would be suitable for dirt track, which meant that in order for Tommy to compete, he'd have to race a motorcycle made by one of his team's direct competitors. Just one week before race day, Tommy got the okay from team manager Mike Preston, who was reluctant to stand in the way of possible history. "He knew I'd been riding with my brothers a lot," Tommy figures, "and he didn't want them to do it without me."

Faced with a tight deadline (and hamstrung by a Kawasaki test at Road America in Wisconsin), Tommy had pulled out the same Yamaha YZ426F that he had raced the previous year (when he'd been on Team Yamaha) and peeled the manufacturer's logos off of the radiator shrouds.

The week spent with Fahie and their friends preparing for Springfield had been like old times for the Haydens, and they'd enjoyed it immensely. "That was probably as much fun as being at the race," Nicky says. "Every night, we were out in the garage burning the midnight oil and ordering parts, getting gas, mounting tires."

Interestingly, all three of the bikes had originally been produced for motocross, not dirt track. Whereas developing technology is welcomed and even demanded in most forms of motorcycle racing, dirt track has always been the exception. Part of this attitude can be traced to the AMA's efforts to keep American manufacturer Harley-Davidson competitive on the big tracks, but one could also accuse dirt track participants of being almost Luddite in their resistance to change. Until recently, AMA National dirt track races were scored entirely by hand, whereas other forms of professional AMA racing (and even some amateur dirt track races) have utilized electronic transponder systems for years.

Although they're simple, traditional dirt trackers are hand-built machines that are expensive to produce. In an early '90s effort to control the costs associated with racing, the AMA had encouraged promoters of amateur short tracks and TTs to adopt a class (called "DTX") for motocrossers—bikes that boasted water-cooled engines, linkage suspension, and hydraulic brakes, and were easily available at any motorcycle dealership. (The bikes were modified with 19-inch wheels and lower suspension, among other changes.) With the pros still running air-cooled Rotax motors in dirt track frames, however, the concept never really caught on, even when Yamaha began producing their YZ400F—the first serious production four-stroke motocrosser—in 1998. The specialty bikes (or "framers," in the sport's parlance) just had too much of a traction advantage on the slippery circuits typical of dirt track. In fact, Tommy's victory at the previous year's Springfield TT was historic in that it had been the inaugural GNC victory for a DTX bike.

Not all circuits are slippery, however, and Springfield's "black gumbo" soil is famous for its traction (the dirt helps make the Springfield Mile the fastest dirt track in the country).

When Tommy had shown up for the facility's inaugural TT in 2001, his Yamaha had raised more than a few eyebrows, but after he held off Nicky's Rotax for the first Grand National dirt track victory by a motocross bike, the tide shifted. In 2002, the pits were filled with motocross machines, and Californian Shaun Russell even had a two-stroke Honda CR250R.

Those pits were pitch-black when the Haydens and their posse rolled into Springfield in the wee hours of Saturday morning. Their arrival wasn't unheralded, as race announcer J. B. Norris recalls: "Talking to Earl going in, I wasn't quite sure if any of them were going to make it, but there was a big buzz about the possibility of the Hayden boys coming. Finally, about three or four days before, it was confirmed that yes, all three of them were going to be there. And they were going to be ready to rock."

The flat track community had a soft spot in its heart for the entire Hayden family. "They got their start in dirt track, so we were always excited to have the Haydens at our races," says IMDA executive director Tommra Luparell. "To have all three of them there, that was really a big deal."

Although there were a few people who resented all the advance attention given to these dirt trackers–turned–road racers, Carr wasn't one of them. "It didn't bother me because it drew attention to flat track," the champ insists. "In the end, that's what we all wanted."

Carr had shown up with a VOR motocross machine, but not long after the 3:00 p.m. start of practice, the Italian bike blew up, leaving the champ on his backup Rotax—one of the few traditional framers on the entry list. Although he wasn't going to roll over for the Haydens, the champ had a feeling history might be made. "If there was any track where it could be done, that was the track," he says. "I knew that it could be possible."

RIGHT: Roger nails the throttle on a corner exit. The youngest Hayden brother had just recovered from a knee injury and very nearly didn't compete at Springfield. "I was pretty nervous," Roger admits, "especially when I looked back and saw Chris Carr behind me." (Flat Trak Fotos) **BELOW:** Employing his signature careful, clean riding style, Tommy heads his aggressive younger brother in the first laps at Springfield. (Flat Trak Fotos)

The Hayden brothers made the June 5, 2002, cover of *Cycle News* for their Springfield podium sweep. A large poster of the cover is the centerpiece on a wall of photos in Earl's home museum in Owensboro. (Chris Jonnum)

Indeed, the circuit, which is always somewhat unpredictable because it is custom-built for each Grand National, seemed made for a motocross bike. The framers—made to turn left—were dragging their exhausts in the main right-hand turn, and the track's two jumps and tight switchback section rewarded the nimble MX bikes.

On a changing track like Springfield's, finishing well in afternoon prequalifying is important, not only because it gets one into the night's program, but also because it gives one an early heat race in relatively smooth conditions. Nicky performed well, setting a record lap time of 1 minute, 53.646 seconds, and by the time pre-qualifying had been completed and a short break instituted, he was ready to go for the main program—so ready, in fact, that when the evening's first heat race lined up at 7:00 p.m., he jumped the flag and had to start from the penalty line. It didn't take Nicky long to negate the penalty, however, and he easily won the heat over JR Schnabel and a host of motocross bikes. Likewise, Tommy dominated heat two, and after Carr took the third qualifier ("I wanted to see at least one dirt track bike win a race tonight—that might be the only one," he said afterward), Roger lined up for the night's final heat race. Ten laps later, the youngest Hayden brother had not only won, but had also captured pole position with the night's fastest heat race—4 minutes, 45.403 seconds, just a couple of tenths faster than Carr's time. So much for Roger Lee being the weak link.

Suddenly, a Hayden sweep looked entirely possible, and the crowd knew it. Covered by an impressive peaked, white awning, the Multi-Purpose Arena's grandstand is relatively small, holding only 4,000 to 5,000 spectators. But dirt track fans are both vocal and knowledgeable, and Norris had done a good job of narrating the story line over the public-address system. As the 18 riders lined up for the main event (15 of them

on motocrossers and 10 on Hondas), the fans rose up off the aluminum bleachers in anticipation.

Tommy timed the start perfectly and pulled the holeshot, with Nicky behind him. Roger was quickly up to third, and when they came by the flag to complete the first of 25 laps, Carr was stuck behind New Yorker Shawn Clark in fifth.

The Haydens were visibly more comfortable than their competitors, the long hours on Earl's replica track having paid off. Also, their recent, plentiful road race experience had been beneficial, allowing them to more quickly come to terms with the TT track's varying corner-radii and right-hand turn. Nicky, in particular, was feeling it: Braking late in the corners, he moved up to Tommy's rear tire and was barely able to contain himself in his relentless efforts to pass his big brother. Just two laps in, that's exactly what he did, nosing by aggressively in the right-hander. From there, as *Cycle News*' Scott Rousseau wrote in his report, "it was *adios hermanos*."

Aware that the track would likely "brush off" (become smoother and more slippery) as the race wore on, and that Tommy was typically stronger in slick conditions, Nicky put his head down and built a small gap, making the most of the ample traction enabled by the IMDA's deft soil preparation. "Anybody who's ridden that track will tell you how good that dirt is," Nicky says.

The scene was set for the Hayden trifecta, but the historic feat wasn't as certain as it seemed. On the first lap, Virginia's Mike Hacker had landed wrong from the kicker jump and slammed his left foot into the ground, badly fracturing his leg. Hacker, sweating from the pain and close to fainting, maintained control as he rolled into the infield and coasted to a

Rose and Earl at the 2002 Springfield TT. "It was my dad's dream," Roger says. "He always talked about how awesome it would be if we got first, second, and third in a race." (Flat Trak Fotos)

stop. The situation arguably called for a red flag, but AMA dirt track manager Bruce Bober refused to stop the race to allow medical personnel to cross the track. Afterward, Hacker took an ambulance ride to St. John's Hospital and underwent a four-hour surgery to have a rod placed in his leg.

Meanwhile, out on the track, Tommy was running out of options. "I tried to stay with [Nicky] for as long as I could, but he was just faster than me, basically," he says.

Technically, it wasn't a very exciting race (were it not for the history factor), with far less passing than had happened the previous year. Realizing that second was as good as it would get that night, Tommy used the track's lane-like configuration to keep tabs on his youngest brother. "Once I got a lead on third, I was just watching Rog and pulling for him," he said.

Roger's bike was near-stock, with a production rear wheel and brakes. He was even running a long motocross front fender, whereas most of the riders had removed theirs or trimmed them down. Carr, the all-time TT winner, was in fourth by this point, but he was beginning to fatigue. He knew that none of the Haydens were campaigning the entire series and that they didn't figure into the points chase, so a top finish wasn't paramount. Still, "I did have thoughts in the back of my mind that I'd like to mess up the family party," he admits.

Tommy closed the gap slightly toward the end, and when Nicky passed the checkers—exultantly punching his fist in the air—his 11-minute, 42.124-second time was 7.697 ticks ahead of Tommy's. Roger came through to complete the fairy-tale ending.

The crowd was in pandemonium, and Nicky was ecstatic, pulling a no-footer wheelie over the big jump on the cool-down lap and then picking up Fahie—armed with the checkered flag—for a victory lap. On the podium, he did a little Kentucky jig, and he sported his trademark ear-to-ear grin as he was interviewed for the telecast of the race. A near-to-tears Nicky stumbled and repeated himself several times, but Tommy was more composed: "I don't know what happened," he joked, his breath fogging in the cool night air. "I think he was sandbagging on me all week!"

With a large group of family members and friends on hand (and parents Earl and Rose beaming now that they were finally able to exhale), the brothers pronounced the night a gift to their sister Jenny, who had graduated from the University of Kentucky a couple weeks earlier, and to Rose, whose birthday was the previous day. (Roger's own birthday was five days later.)

"Usually, races are all individual accomplishments," Tommy said later. "With this one, I didn't win the race, so I didn't really have that thrill, but it was really rewarding in a different kind of way, with all of us having a kind of group success at the same time. It was kind of like a team sport, almost."

There was a similar feeling of solidarity among the fortunate spectators, who left the track that night knowing they'd not only witnessed history being made, but that they'd gotten a sneak peek at the future of American motorcycle racing, both in terms of machinery (every National TT since has been won by a motocross-based bike), and riders (all the Hayden brothers have since accomplished other great feats).

"Having three brothers finish on the podium is something that had never happened before," says the IMDA's Luparell, "and it probably won't happen again. So of course it's an honor that it happened at our track and our event."

Such an honor, in fact, that since May 26, 2002, the Illinois State Fairgrounds' Multi-Purpose Arena has been unofficially known—among motorcycle racing fans, at least—as Hayden Hollow.

BELOW: For those not in the know, it might not look like anything particularly special, but this is a truly historic victory podium. Never before had an AMA professional-racing rostrum been completely occupied by one family. (Shogo Nakao) **RIGHT:** Nicky pulls a celebratory wheelie as the checkers wave. Moments later, history would be made as Tommy and then Roger crossed the line. (Flat Trak Fotos)

CHAPTER 2

A FAMILY FROM OWENSBORO

Tommy shows off a pair of his old Earl's Racing Team leathers in the family's original garage. (Chris Jonnum)

For Thomas Earl Hayden and Rose Marie Kamuf, the Owensboro City Jail was not so much an inauspicious first meeting place as it was an unlikely one. The two high schoolers were basically good kids, and an evening in lockup for possession of alcohol by a minor was anything but typical for either of them. The fact that the two were both so obviously out of place may be why they immediately hit it off, and after that night, Earl and Rose made a point of meeting regularly in some of their hometown's more agreeable locales.

Located near Kentucky's northwest border, on the banks of the Ohio River, Owensboro is known best for its barbecue (the biggest civic event is the annual International Bar-B-Q Festival, and President Clinton famously ate at the town's Moonlite Bar-B-Q Inn). Celebrity natives include actor Johnny Depp; NBA player Rex Chapman; NFL player Mark Higgs; Major League Baseball player Brad Wilkerson; and NASCAR drivers Jeremy Mayfield, Jeff and David Green, and Darrell and Michael Waltrip. Back in the late '60s and early '70s, though, as Earl courted Rose, the couple was more interested in two-wheel sport. Not a lot has changed.

Earl had caught the motorcycle bug in 1964, when his school bus would stop every day in front of a Honda shop. After getting his own bike, Earl began competing in local enduros, scrambles, and dirt track races, and he immediately knew that he had found his passion—if not exactly his calling ("I had a lot of nerve and not much talent," he admits). A typical date with Rose consisted of a trip to the races.

Fortunately, Rose enjoyed the scene and the characters that went with it nearly as much as Earl did. Soon, she was racing as well, her horse-riding experience negating any handicap for lack of motorcycle seat time. For five years, she went undefeated in the Powder Puff class, her first loss coming via a career-ending crash. (She was already in the ambulance by the time Earl made his way to the scene, but the EMTs were kind enough to reload her so he could snap a photo.) Earl was anything but jealous of Rose's racing success. "The way I figure it, it's

Earl feeds Rose a piece of cake at their wedding reception. Wearing his signature soul patch on his chin even in 1976, Earl is no trend-chasing Johnny-come-lately! (Hayden collection)

about bloodlines," he says with a laugh. "I needed to catch a Thoroughbred, because I'm not that fast!"

Children were indeed a priority for Earl and Rose, both of whom come from very large families. "I've always been around kids," Rose says. "I can deal with kids better than I can a lot of grown-ups; they've got a whole lot more sense."

After nearly a decade of dating, when they were 30 and 26, respectively, Earl and Rose were married on February 21, 1976. Two years, four months, and 21 days later, Thomas Earl II—the first of the Hayden children—was born in Daviess County Hospital.

Upstairs from the living room in the Hayden household on Earl's Lane, across from a shallow balcony loaded with racing trophies the size of an average human, is a small bedroom with low, slanted ceilings. The wallpaper has a motorcycle motif, but it's almost completely obscured by posters, magazine photographs, and other racing memorabilia: an autographed No. 1 plate from Scott Parker's 1999 Grand National farewell tour (signed to Roger Lee); photos of Ronnie Jones, Jimmy Filice, Bubba Shobert, Jeremy McGrath, Larry Pegram, Will Davis, Doug Chandler (dirt track and road race versions), Doug Henry, and others; and a note written by a young Nicky, reading "Bones heal. Pain is temporary. Glory lasts forever." Against one wall sits a small bookcase, its shelves filled with photo albums that are in

turn filled with racing pictures. This was the bedroom of the young Hayden brothers.

Tommy became the room's first resident at just a few months of age, shortly after he and his parents moved into the house. (Earl and Rose still own and rent out their original dwelling, which is just a mile away on Wayside Drive.) Mom and dad had both been raised in rural settings—Rose on the outskirts of Owensboro, and Earl on a 60-acre farm in nearby Newman—and they'd been after something similar when choosing their "new" home (the majority of which was actually built in the 19th century). "It's got leaks and the floors aren't that level," Earl says, "but I'd much rather have this than some fancy house in the city."

Fields and corrals surround the residence, and upon moving in, the young couple started a small horse-breeding business, though it wasn't long before Rose's frequent pregnancies prevented her from completing her Thoroughbred-exercising duties. Tommy's arrival was followed about two years later by the birth of Jennifer Rose, and Nicholas Patrick greeted the world on July 30, 1981, becoming a roommate with Tommy as soon as he was out of a crib. Roger Lee joined the family on May 30, 1983 (later replacing Tommy in the room at age 6), and three years after his birth, Kathleen Marie became the fifth and final Hayden child.

Earl knew from the start that he wanted to give his children the opportunity to be successful motorcycle racers, and he realized from his own frequent crashes that good balance was paramount. The kids had a plastic play horse, with a spring at each corner attaching it to a metal frame. Once each Hayden child was able to sit on the toy and rock, Earl would remove one of the four springs; when they had that mastered, he'd remove the spring from the opposite corner. Balancing with just two springs was extremely difficult, but the children quickly caught on.

LEFT: A dapper Nicky collects his prized third-place jacket at the Western Kentucky Cycle Racing Association year-end banquet. Earl and Rose always made a point of dressing the kids well for these functions, figuring potential sponsors appreciated it. (Hayden collection) BELOW: Earl poses with four of his five kids (from left), Roger, Kathleen, Nicky, and Tommy, and their bicycles in the driveway. Nicky is wearing a T-shirt from the Beauty Shack, a local hair salon that sponsored him for a short time. Note Roger's zip-tied number plate. (Hayden collection)

Using a slightly oversize YZ80, Earl helps Nicky get used to the concept of shifting in the front yard on Earl's Lane. (Hayden collection)

Nicky steers his dirt track-framed YZ80 through a turn in Marion, Kentucky; the Hayden trailer is in the background. Nicky is wearing baseball batting gloves, as it was impossible for Earl and Rose to find motorcycle gloves in a small-enough size. (Hayden collection)

Where it all started: The Haydens' first race trailer, originally designed for snowmobiles, was purchased from an uncle. Sometimes during the winter breaks, when the kids missed being at the races, they'd camp out in the trailer in the front yard. (Hayden collection)

Meanwhile, the Haydens' fields soon came to be used more for motorcycle riding than horse training. Earl had given up his breeding endeavors to open a used-car dealership called 2nd Chance Auto, and although he kept a few ponies and even added some llamas and a potbellied pig named Rudy, all of the animals had to stay clear of the minibikes that ruled the property.

Tommy was riding shortly after he could walk, and racing by age 3, his first competition coming at an Owensboro $3/8$ Mile called Windy Hollow Raceway Park. A couple of years later, Paducah International Raceway's $3/8$ Mile clay oval became the site of Jenny and Nicky's first race. Soon, all three older siblings were competing regularly—a turn of events that felt completely natural to the Haydens. "Earl raced, so when we had kids, then they raced too," Rose says matter-of-factly. "I didn't really think it was a big to-do. It was something we did as a family."

In the evenings, Earl would tell bedtime stories about races involving American road racing legends like Kenny Roberts and Wayne Rainey, weaving his kids into the tales. If he ended a story without a Hayden victory, the kids would ask him to retell it until they had won.

The Hayden home's isolated setting meant there weren't many "normal" children around with whom the Hayden kids could play or compare themselves. "It was as simple a life as you could get," Tommy recalls. "We probably spent 99 percent of our time at home. We were a big family with similar interests, and it wasn't like we had to go somewhere to find something to do or someone to play with."

Most of the kids' friends were made at the racetracks, so the Hayden children naturally assumed that all kids rode motorcycles. Although there weren't many other girls competing, Jenny made friends with her competitors' sisters. "My broth-ers were doing it," Jenny says of racing, "so it was just kind of something that we did."

Because the small bikes were relatively light, Jenny wasn't at much of a physical disadvantage, and she would regularly win races and make the podium. Some parents didn't like their kids losing to a girl and would complain, but most people were fine with her racing.

Things were different for the two younger Hayden siblings. Roger—perhaps daunted by an early crash into a tree on the Hayden ranch and a separate motorcycle mishap with one of Earl's horses—didn't initially have much of an interest in racing, and his parents didn't force him. "I can remember going to the races and him just being there playing in the back of the box van," Nicky says.

Finally, when he reached age 6 (by which time Tommy had already been racing for eight years), Roger decided to start competing, in part so he could miss school more often. His first race was at an indoor flat track in Ohio, and he won on a Yamaha PW50. Still, playing continued to take precedence, at least initially, and Roger could occasionally be spotted trying valiantly to unlap himself after missing the start of an eighth-lap heat race. After a few years, he began getting more serious.

Kathleen raced 50s for a while as well, but soon decided that motorcycle racing wasn't for her. "Being the fifth child, I was getting the hand-me-downs," she explains. "I remember there were several races back-to-back, where I'd practice and then my bike wouldn't start for the race. About that time, I just decided to quit the racing thing and stick with balls and bats. Looking back, I wish that I rode a little bit more, but I took a different path."

Kathleen still enjoyed going to the races and playing with her dolls in the pits. Again, this was fine with her parents; Earl had enough experience to know that between the travel and

the injuries, the racing life could be a rough one. Neither he nor Rose wanted to force that on any of their children, and they wanted the ones who *did* race to eventually be well-compensated for it.

"If we were going to do it, I wanted us to do it right and not just for a hobby," Earl says. "It's okay to race for fun, but why not make a good living at it? If everyone loved what they did for a living, maybe we wouldn't have so many problems in this world."

Earl built a small dirt oval and a TT track in the field on the west side of the house, and when the kids weren't in school or at a race, that's where they could usually be found. They'd often log four hours a day on the bikes, usually riding until it was dark, prompting the family to name the field Sunset Downs.

Not all of the kids' riding time was spent on their tracks. If it rained, they'd do laps around the planter in the asphalt driveway, and they'd sometimes pair up and organize relay races around the property. They'd ride anything—bicycles, mini dirt trackers, Honda Z50s and XR80s and 100s, even three-wheelers and go-karts.

Eventually, Earl brought home a Yamaha YSR50 mini road racer that the kids would take turns riding in the driveway. One rainy day, they decided to organize a mock Suzuka 8 Hours endurance race: They fixed up their shed like a pit-row garage at the famous Japanese circuit, established a rider

order, clicked the stopwatch, and started riding. As the hours passed, the laps around the short driveway accumulated, and just like at the real Suzuka, they continued riding even after it got dark. Finally, Roger crashed, sliding so far on the wet asphalt that he nearly collided with the garage, bringing a premature end to the adventure.

The Hayden kids certainly weren't wanting for imagination, a fact that came in handy during unacceptably long layoffs between real races. In such circumstances, they'd take matters into their own hands, piling their "motorcycles" (bicycles) into the "box trailer" (a wooden pallet), and pulling it behind their "race van" (Earl's sit-down lawnmower). After traveling to the end of the driveway, they'd pull over, switch drivers, and return to the house, where they'd unload and prepare their pit area. Even details like sign-up and tech inspection were included in their fantasies.

Sometimes, the Hayden kids' home races were a bit less make-believe: Earl made a point of ending each day with a formal "play race," complete with a checkered flag that the winner got to "pack" on a victory lap. Although he forbade the kids from performing elaborate victory celebrations ("Most show-offs aren't very fast," he'd say), Earl figured a lap with the checkers was an appropriate reward for a win. Besides, the ritual helped nurture the kids' competitive instincts; during the victory lap, Earl sometimes did all he could do to prevent the kids who hadn't won from tackling the victor.

As long as it didn't go too far, Earl saw this competitiveness as a good thing. He had begun reading biographies on great champions—racing heroes like Dick Mann, Gary Nixon, and Bart Markel, but also stick-and-ball athletes like Pete Rose, Earvin "Magic" Johnson, and Larry Bird—and his studies led him to conclude that top sportsmen all shared the same attributes: talent, good work habits, and passion,

Nicky is at the wheel of his lawnmower "race van," while Roger rides with the bikes in the pallet "trailer." The German shepherd is one in a line of guard dogs Earl kept, each named Tilly. They protected the motorcycles and occasionally scared visitors onto their car hoods. (Hayden collection)

but most important, an intense desire to win. This was also evident when the family would watch sports on television.

"We'd watch a championship game, and the guys on the team that lost would be so down that you'd think they finished 20th or something," Earl remembers. "These guys were better than any other team except one, but they were still sad. That's how bad they wanted it."

Earl would point this out to his kids, and they easily noticed the contrast between those players and their own competitors, who would celebrate a fifth-place trophy at a local race like they had won the World Championship. Meanwhile, Tommy, Jenny, and Nicky were collecting first-place trophies and championship jackets from the Western Kentucky Competition Racing Association (WKCRA)—a local circuit that hit all the area's county fairs and comprised most the Hayden family's race schedule.

Earl had made friends with Jim Pegram, the father of Ohio dirt tracker Larry Pegram, who would sometimes come down and practice on the Haydens' track with fellow Ohio native Scott Stump. Those two riders were five and eight years older than Tommy, so these occasions were good opportunities for the Hayden kids to pick up some pointers.

The Haydens also liked to go watch the pros in action when the opportunity would arise. Every summer, Earl and Rose would drive the kids three-and-a-half hours to the Indiana State Fair, where they'd take in the fair during the day and then watch the Indy Mile at night. After their 1984 visit to that race, they drove home with their first real dirt track bikes, which they purchased from the Roeders—another dirt track family whose kids were older than the Hayden boys. Both of the bikes had belonged to Jessie (the youngest Roeder but six years older than Tommy); one was a Yamaha 60 in a dirt track frame that had been hand-built by Roeder patriarch Geo Sr., and the other was a Yamaha 80 in a Viper monoshock frame.

Both bikes were very fast, but Tommy and Nicky had some trouble adapting to them at first. Tommy, now 6, could barely touch the ground on the 80, and Earl had to hold him up on the starts. Still just 3, Nicky hadn't yet learned to shift, and the first time he got on the 60, he took off in first gear and held the throttle wide open until the engine seized. Once they got the hang of the new bikes, however, their results began to get even better.

Despite the family's success, and the seriousness with which they approached racing, Earl and Rose never got upset on the occasions when their children lost. "We just wanted them to give 100 percent," Rose says. "If they did that and they got beat, then they got beat."

In fact, the Haydens even imposed a sort of handicap on themselves: When applying for the kids' AMA cards, Earl had exaggerated the ages of Tommy and Nicky by one year and two years, respectively. This was mainly to enable them to start racing earlier (the AMA had an age minimum), but it also helped the boys improve quickly by facing older, more experienced competitors. Sure, winning now was nice, but it was more important to the Haydens to work toward winning in the future.

The Haydens were fairly devout Catholics, and when they were on the road on Sundays, they'd try to find a local church and attend mass along with the Pegrams. When they were home, they'd spend Sunday mornings at Owensboro's Precious Blood Catholic Church, whose small, private elementary school the kids also attended, making the mile trip through local fields on their motorcycles and leaning them against the school fence. With each grade level comprising only about 15 children and a total student body of only about 75 kids, the school didn't offer much in the way of social options, and the Haydens frequently missed class to attend races (something that was easier to do at Precious Blood than it would have been at a public school). The boys played some sports, but they often had to skip games to go racing, and anyway, the school teams were terrible. For the most part, the Hayden kids continued to spend their free time on Earl's Lane.

"We didn't really hang out with kids from our school," Nicky says. "We weren't exactly outsiders, but we didn't go hang out at the local pool or park like most kids did." Considering all the motorcycles the Hayden family owned, it's no surprise that the few friends they did have—mainly just Eric Reynolds back then—liked to come to their house as well.

"For show and tell, I'd bring Matchbox toy cars," Reynolds says, "whereas Nicky would be bringing in trophies from a race the weekend before. It was a lot of fun at their house, and they'd let me ride their bikes and stuff."

Early on, Nicky had been diagnosed with dyslexia and was held back a grade to attend special classes for overcoming the learning disorder. He soon licked the problem, but between struggling with the class work and his tendency toward mischief, he continued to have difficulties in school.

After one particular term that had gone better than usual, Nicky came home and proudly showed his parents his report card. "These are good grades, but what about this mark for bad conduct?" Rose asked.

"Okay, now listen," Nicky replied seriously. "I'm not going to be able to do both. You guys are going to have to make a choice: grades or conduct?" Earl and Rose looked at each other and chuckled, agreeing that if this was the case, they'd take the good grades.

Missing school for races didn't help matters, and the middle school teachers were less understanding. "They thought we were blowing our lives," Roger says. "They'd say, 'What are you going to do when you have to get a job? How are you going to make a living?'"

"Our parents used to hear it from some of our teachers," Tommy adds. "It didn't look good for them to be taking their kids out of school for a week to ride motorcycles at Daytona Bike Week. Some of the teachers were supportive, but others didn't understand how seriously we were taking it, or what the potential was."

It wasn't only the teachers who didn't approve of Earl and Rose's choices for their children. The Haydens were no strangers to the local emergency room, and the doctors objected when they'd hear that the kids had sustained their injuries in motorcycle crashes.

Not that Earl and Rose were overly eager to have the kids visit the doctor. Once at a race in Florida, Roger got knocked down and didn't immediately get back to his feet. The ambulance crew came to check him out, and the EMTs said that he would have to be taken in for X-rays. Earl would hear nothing of it: "I don't see any bones sticking through the skin," Earl said, "but if he needs to go to the hospital, then I'll take him myself. Otherwise, we're going racing." (Sure enough, Roger lined back up for the restart and won the race.)

Still, there were enough emergency-room visits that it eventually got to the point where the doctors would stall or even refuse to treat the Haydens, so the kids soon learned to say they'd been hurt riding a bicycle or a skateboard. The Haydens had chosen their path, and they weren't about to let a bump in the road cause a detour. Their adventures were only bringing them closer as a family, and the Hayden kids were starting to make a mark.

BELOW: Tommy, Nicky, and Roger spent a considerable chunk of their childhood in this poster-covered bedroom. Beyond the far door was the sisters' bedroom. The albums in the bookcase contain many of the photos used in this book. (Chris Jonnum)

LEFT: Racing photos and memorabilia dominate Earl's crowded office at 2nd Chance Auto. Even with his busy travel schedule and three kids with factory rides, the Hayden patriarch continues to run his business. (Chris Jonnum)

CHAPTER 3 THE DREAM YEARS

FAR LEFT: The *Motorcycle Man* album that inspired the Haydens: The songs were written by Melva Murphy and were sung by Buddy Mize. Murphy, whose husband worked for Yamaha, also did oil paintings of the riders. Then–AMA executive director Russ March gave Murphy permission to use the AMA logo, with the stipulation that the AMA receive a quantity of records to sell. The album was released around 1971, and as former AMA president Ed Youngblood notes, "I don't think we moved too many." (Chris Jonnum)

LEFT: Shortly after arriving home from the 1991 Amateur Nationals in Illinois, Nicky, Tommy, and Roger show off their trophy haul, including No. 1 plates in the 85cc, 250cc, and 65cc classes, respectively. (Hayden collection)

OPPOSITE: Earl straightens Roger's Kiwi cap for a trophy photo following a day at the Henry, Illinois, half mile during the Amateur Nationals. Kiwi was an early helmet sponsor for the Haydens, and Earl always wanted to be sure the kids represented such supporters well. (Hayden collection) **ABOVE:** With the sun going down on a day of racing at the 1987 Amateur Nationals in Elkhorn, Wisconsin, Tommy displays his No. 1 plate from the 80cc 7-11 half-mile event. Also in the photo are Nicky, Earl, and family friend Darrell "Tater Tot" Stallings. (Hayden collection)

One day while flipping through a motorcycle magazine, Earl came across an advertisement for a record album called *Motorcycle Man: The True Story of Motorcycles*. He filled out the order form and put a check in the mail, and a few weeks later, a package showed up at Earl's Lane. The album had an AMA logo on the cover, along with a painting of Bart Markel leading a pack of dirt trackers around a corner. Intrigued, he flipped it over. On the back were black-and-white photos of racers like Markel, Mark Brelsford, Cal Rayborn, Gary Nixon, and Gene Romero.

Earl put the album on the turntable, which began emitting homespun songs with titles like "Panic in the Pits," "Grandstand Granny," and "Cycle Racin' Man." Interspersed between the quirky tunes were spoken-word bits romanticizing life on the Grand National dirt track circuit. Although their musical talents were open to question, singer Buddy Mize and songwriter Melva Murphy obviously knew a thing or two about motorcycle racing.

That was enough for Earl, who recorded the album onto a cassette tape and stuck it in the race van. On the family's next trip, as they neared the racetrack, Earl popped the tape into the stereo. The kids couldn't believe what they were hearing. From that day on, the Haydens would always listen to *Motorcycle Man* whenever they got close to the track, and Earl would give out copies to sponsors as thank-you gifts. By the latter half of the '80s, the album was getting quite a workout.

Dirt track racing's fundamentals couldn't be more basic—meet up at a flat, dirt oval; line up on a chalk line; and race around for a predetermined number of laps, left feet shod in steel shoes that slide along the smooth clay. Even the bikes are relatively simple, changing little from year to year. And in keeping with the theme of simplicity, the people who compete in dirt track tend to be uncomplicated and down-to-earth.

This was the setting in which the Haydens spent much of their time as the kids were growing up, traveling to races around the

Midwest—dirt track's birthplace—and spending time together as a family. "When I think about growing up, those are the years that I think about," Jenny says. "We were always going somewhere, racing every single weekend."

The ritual would begin every March, when the family would celebrate the end to the cold winter months by heading down to Florida for the amateur events at Daytona Bike Week—one of the year's biggest races and a chance to see the pros in action. After that, they'd hit the WKCRA circuit for several months until it was time for July's AMA Amateur National Dirt Track—the biggest race of the year and a rare opportunity to race on good tracks against the best riders from around the country. Classes were broken down by age, displacement, and skill level, and championships were awarded in the specialties of short track, half-mile, mile, and TT.

Tommy first competed in the race at age 8, in 1987, when it was held in Illinois. The family opted not to travel to Washington State for the following year's event, but the next summer the Amateur Nationals returned to Illinois, and they would remain at the historic Peoria venue for four years. Tommy, Jenny, and Nicky all raced in '89, with Roger joining in a couple years later.

The Haydens were quick learners. In 1989, Tommy, Nicky, and Jenny had that 65cc TT-class podium sweep that was a precursor of the Hayden brothers' 2002 domination of the Springfield TT GNC rostrum. "That was fun," Earl says. "That race and the Springfield TT podium are my two most memorable races."

That same week, Roger was competing in a 50cc race, and when he didn't come back to the pits afterward, Earl and Rose went looking for him. They found him in a creek that skirts the track. "He had run off the track on the last lap, and we didn't see him!" Earl says with a laugh.

In '91, Nicky won five of his six classes, losing the half-mile to Glenn "JR" Schnabel when the race was red-flagged. ("I'm still bitter about that," he says now.)

Whereas Nicky often faced Schnabel and Bryan Bigelow, Tommy's main rival was Kenny Coolbeth. (All three of these rivals were fast amateurs who have since found success on the Grand National Championship circuit.) Roger got his start at the Amateur Nationals in '91, when he borrowed another kid's fast 50. The highly modified bike failed to finish two races, and when it finally did reach the finish line, it didn't pass post-race tech inspection. Roger's results would soon improve as well, however, despite tough competition from Bryan Smith (currently a pro dirt tracker), Toby Jorgensen (who would be tragically killed in a crash at the 1999 Dallas Mile GNC), and Tony Meiring (now a racer on the AMA Superbike circuit).

Winning was obviously the main focus for the Haydens, but when it came to the Amateur Championships, the racing was only part of what the kids looked forward to. Equally important was the social aspect. "It was always a lot of fun," Nicky says. "It seemed like all the families would stay at the same hotel, and everybody would be riding bicycles, or in the swimming pool, or having water-balloon fights, or working on their bikes in the parking lot, or riding their pit bikes down the hallway—lots of good memories."

With the Haydens consistently doing quite well (sometimes winning every class between them), it wasn't unusual for them to lose a few of those friends by the time the weekend was over. Sometimes, parents would complain that the Haydens won because they had money, but the truth was that their equipment was far from the best on the track. With four kids racing, the family would regularly hand bikes down from child to child. Roger's motorcycles were sometimes worn out by the time he got them, and since Tommy was a sort of unofficial guinea pig for the family, his setups were often far from perfect (particularly bad

BELOW: Earl bought this 1989 Ford box van from pro racer Scott Stump in 1991, and the family used it for years. "It had a custom sleeper over the front, with a TV in it," Nicky recalls. "There was a Super Mario game we used to play on the way to the races, and we had two movies we could watch: *Ace Ventura* and *Dirty Dancing*. That last one was my mom's." (Hayden collection)

RIGHT: Nicky (second row, right) and Roger (bottom row, second from right) pose for their grade school baseball team photo. "We were pretty terrible," Nicky admits. (Hayden collection)

Jenny throws a leg over Tommy's first dirt track-framed bike, a 60cc Yamaha purchased from the Roeder family, while one of the Tillys checks out another machine. Note the Gary Nixon helmet and the lawn chairs ready to be loaded up for the next race. (Hayden collection)

was his air-cooled 250, aboard which he had to race the much-faster water-cooled bikes of his competitors). This scenario sometimes—but not always—resulted in Nicky getting the best of the deal. His first-ever brand-new bike, a 1991 Yamaha YZ80 that boasted 16-inch wheels and lowered suspension, was almost unbeatable, even after he passed it down to Roger.

Nor could the Hayden kids' success be put down to skilled tuning; Earl (or "Squirrel," as the boys had taken to calling him) was too busy to do much work on the bikes, and anyway, he really wasn't a very good mechanic. Fortunately, Tommy proved to be handy with a wrench, and in the early years, he was doing much of the bike maintenance himself. "I'd say by the time Tommy was 8 or 9, he was a better mechanic than my dad," Nicky says.

Tommy didn't do all of the mechanical work, as the Haydens also got help from family friends. Buddies like Reynolds Wrap could always be counted on to run a pit board or push a bike to the line, but for real tuning help, they worked first with Jerry Clark (who owned a shop in town) and later Recil Hart. Recil was the son of Marlin Hart (who had raced at the same events Earl had back in the day and owned a race team). A former expert dirt tracker himself, Recil was a few years older than Tommy. Earl knew he needed help keeping the bikes running, so they worked out a deal whereby Recil would live with the Haydens—rooming with Tommy—and earn his keep and a ride to the races by working on the family's many motorcycles. "They were a little out of control at that time, but Recil whipped them into shape," Marlin remembers.

Recil acted as a sort of big brother to the Hayden kids, teaching them to work on their bikes and giving them racing advice. Although Recil had the Hayden kids under control, he did occasionally have his hands full with other, disgruntled

parents, who sometimes reacted to defeat by accusing the Haydens of cheating.

This was well before the Haydens had added the modern garage, where they would one day prepare for the 2002 Springfield TT, so most of the work was done in their small, wood-panel-lined shop, located across the driveway from the house. It wasn't exactly luxurious, but to the Hayden kids, it was a factory race shop, and they did their best to outfit it as such: Against one wall, a modest workbench sat on two file cabinets, and plywood shelves held oil cans, trophies, stacks of sprockets, and tackle boxes filled with spark plugs and spare brake and shift levers. A solvent tank sat on a metal drum in the corner, with a line of K&N air filters drying on a ledge above it. A door in the back accessed a tiny space that Tommy fixed up as a parts room, with exhaust pipes hanging above rows of tires. On a sheet of paper taped to one wall, the lap records for Sunset Downs were tracked. In this domain, Tommy, his brothers, and Recil would sit the bikes on stands in the center of the linoleum floor and work until Rose came in and dragged them to bed.

Race announcer Donny Bargmann hands Nicky the microphone for a post–80cc TT victory speech during the 1991 Amateur Nationals in Peoria. Several other future Grand National riders appear, including Bryan Bigelow and JR Schnabel (to Nicky's right and left, respectively). (Hayden collection)

Eventually, Recil returned to racing, and his dad began helping the Hayden boys in his place. One trip to the Amateur Nationals stands out in his mind. "Their bikes all broke down, and I had to work on them big-time," Marlin remembers. "I told Earl, 'When we get home, we're going to sell these yard-sale models and build some *real* motorcycles.'"

Marlin prepared the brothers a few Rotaxes and painted "Hart Racing" on the fuel tanks, and their results started getting even better. The elder Hart would race-prep the bikes, take them to the events, then drive all night to get the kids home in time for school on Monday. "I enjoyed it, and Earl always paid me," Marlin says. "He's a great old boy, and the mother Rose is just a first-class lady."

By this time, the Haydens had accumulated quite a collection of bikes. Jess Roeder remembers the Haydens showing up at races with "about 20 motorcycles" piled in their van. "They'd load the bottom row first, and then they'd have to load the others on top of them to fit them all in there," he says with a laugh. "There were so many [Hayden kids] coming up, it was tough to keep track of who was who. You just knew that if they were a Hayden, then they were fast."

To make matters more confusing, the Hayden kids all ran the same racing number. Earl had worn No. 69 back in his racing days ("I crashed often enough that I needed something you could read upside-down," he explains), so that's what Tommy

had chosen when he started competing. With bikes being handed down from sibling to sibling, it was easiest to just have Jenny, Nicky, and Roger run the same number. When one bike wouldn't start, its owner could just grab whatever was next to it; it wasn't unusual to see Nicky trying to qualify for the 80cc main on Jenny's 60cc!

Apart from their menagerie of bikes, the Haydens didn't exactly live high on the hog. One year, after they'd packed their bags for Daytona, Earl had to place buckets around the living room to catch water from a leaky roof. Any vacation time was dedicated to racing, and neither parent ever had fancy transportation; Rose used the race van to get around Owensboro, and to this day, Nicky says that apart from rental vehicles, he's never seen Earl drive a car worth more than $1,000.

Perhaps that's just as well, given Earl's penchant for fender-benders. When the Haydens eventually upgraded to a box van, it didn't take him long to run it into a low overhang at a restaurant, resulting in the van's roof leaking whenever it rained. On another occasion, the wiring system caught fire, and although Earl managed to put out the flames fairly quickly, the electrics were never quite right after that. Neither the air conditioning nor the heater worked, and a malfunctioning fuel gauge—along with Earl's traditional push to make it to the Indiana border (where the diesel cost less)—resulted in a prematurely empty fuel tank on more than one occasion.

The Hayden kids would often bring a friend or two along on their trips, and with so many kids packed into the van, it wasn't uncommon for Earl and Rose to forget one at a restaurant and have to double back. That said, restaurant stops weren't a given; many meals—hamburgers, sandwiches, and chicken salad—were prepared by Rose prior to every race and packed for the trip. The family also had a couple of fishing rods stashed in the van, and sometimes they'd camp at pay lakes and catch their dinner. (Once, Roger hooked a duck that

With as many as five kids racing at times, the family's Ford van could get pretty crowded. Here it is loaded down for the trip to the Amateur Nationals. The white bike with No. 69J belongs to Jenny. (Hayden collection)

belonged to the lake owner, and it put up such a squawk that he threw down his pole and ran. "I had kind of wanted to do it," he admits now, "but once it happened, I changed my mind because the thing went wild.")

When the Haydens stopped at restaurants, water was the only beverage allowed. Family members and anyone else that had come along to help out would usually share a single, budget hotel room. If it got a little overcrowded, some people would stay in the box van, where there was a couch and a bunk bed, and then take advantage of the hotel shower the next day. On most mornings, the whole crew would partake of the free continental breakfasts, and it was Nicky's job to fill up the cooler from the hotel ice machine.

When Rose and the girls weren't along, the Hayden males looked forward to spending race weekends camping in the van at the racetrack or at a local campground. The boys liked to invite a friend on these trips, and when there was free time they would bring a football to toss around, their bicycles to ride, and their fishing poles in case there was a lake or pond nearby. It was a good way for them to mix in some normal, fun, kid stuff with the seriousness of racing. Their favorite part of the camping experience was making their signature camp breakfasts, which they're still proud of. These involved throwing whatever food they had—ingredients like eggs, bacon, ham, sausage, cheese, and potatoes—into a frying pan and mixing it all together. The meals were mostly eaten with a shared fork and washed down with milk straight out of the carton. It was anything but fine dining, but the Haydens loved it.

It wasn't that the Haydens were hard up financially. By now, Earl had added a car-dealership to the carwash business and his property-rental enterprise, so, technically, the family's income was comfortably middle-class. They were doing well enough that all five Hayden children wore braces (although Earl tried to work the orthodontist for

a package deal), but with four kids competing in multiple racing classes, the Haydens were spending a small fortune on entry fees.

Earl also still had a few horses, but they were there more as a distraction for Jenny than to make money. "Earl was always trying to get her off of bikes and onto horses," Larry Pegram remembers. "He'd always say she couldn't ride after she was 10, and then it was after she was 12. It kept going up. He and Rose were just worried about her, but she was every bit as good as the boys were."

Ironically, one of the horses bucked Jenny off once when Pegram was visiting in 1989, and she broke her arm in the fall. "Earl came out and made us ride that horse until it was about dead, to punish it for hurting her," Pegram says. "Then he sold it the next day."

Earl and Rose's concern wasn't completely without basis. While riding Tommy's 125 at Kentucky's Hopkinsville Speedway, in just her third race on a full-size bike, Jenny got into a high-speed wobble on a straightaway and went down hard, breaking several bones. Following that experience, she began asking herself what kind of a future she had with motorcycle racing.

"The boys had always thought that they would go on and be professionals, and that that was what they would do with their lives," Jenny says. "Me, I had never anticipated that.

Jenny leads Tommy, Nicky, and the rest of the 65cc TT class during the 1989 AMA Amateur Nationals, where the siblings swept the podium. "I felt like I wanted to beat the other riders more than I did my brothers," Jenny says. (Hayden collection)

I wanted to go to college and do those kinds of things, and it was too expensive to do if I wasn't committed."

Earl and Rose weren't completely disappointed when their oldest daughter talked about hanging up her helmet. Jenny didn't want to end it on a bad note, however, so she continued competing for another year before finally calling it quits.

Jenny missed competing after she stopped, but because Tommy, Nicky, and Roger were all still so involved in the sport, she still had plenty of reasons for attending races. With her newfound free time, she immediately started getting into tennis, and in that sport—as in life—her years racing motorcycles proved invaluable. "I think sometimes females grow up thinking males are better than them," says Jenny, who still keeps in touch with the friends she made in her racing days. "I've never felt like that. Also, racing helped me to be closer to my brothers; if I hadn't raced, I don't know if I'd have ever talked to them!"

Although Jenny was now on the sidelines, the Hayden boys were now racing more than ever. They had even begun racing occasionally during the cold winter months, hitting indoor races that took place on tiny, polished-concrete ovals. Since they lacked an AMA sanction, these events (called "outlaw" races) used a "run what ya brung" format and didn't have age limits, so the Hayden kids got a chance to go head-to-head against older riders on faster bikes. Even better, these races often offered modest cash prizes, so they could sometimes come close to breaking even.

Motorcycle racing consumed the boys' lives to such an extent that it didn't leave room for normal young-man interests like stick-and-ball sports. Nicky and Roger did dabble with Pop Warner football, playing a little for a successful team called the Colts, but it was really little more than a diversion. Similarly, girls were viewed primarily as a distraction;

the occasional flirtation was fine, but steady girlfriends were rare. This became more difficult as females began to take an intense interest in the Haydens. (Dirt track announcer J. B. Norris, who was then an ad manager for *American Motorcyclist* magazine, remembers that his daughter Megan and her two friends—all of whom were trophy girls—each had a Hayden brother "picked out.")

With the Haydens' crazy travel schedule and obvious dedication to racing, it wasn't uncommon for parents to accuse Earl and Rose of putting undue pressure on their children. The truth is that by then, the motivation was coming mostly from the brothers themselves, and if Earl was to blame for anything, it was for instilling in his kids such a strong hunger for success. "I didn't *have* to pressure them to race," Earl says. "Maybe to brush their teeth or to do their homework, but never to race."

In fact, on occasions when the boys would act up in school, Earl would sometimes present as a threat the possibility of *not* racing, warning that he'd keep the family home from Daytona, say, if Nicky or Roger didn't turn things around. Not that those threats carried much weight: "They knew dang good and well that their father wouldn't stick to it," Rose says, "but they would straighten up."

Perhaps not surprisingly, the boys were on their best behavior when they were either at a race or traveling to one. "They were sweethearted kids," Marlin Hart says. "You'd tell them to shower at the hotel in the morning, and boy, they'd get showered and dressed and be sitting on the bed when their mother and father come in the door to get them. They were just like soldiers. They weren't interested in anything but racing."

The bottom line is that if the Hayden boys were missing out on anything, they certainly didn't mind. Their lives were fantasy material for most young men, and their considerable success was thanks more to their parents' love and support than to any pressure that was placed on them.

Early Hayden sponsor-manager Cliff Sherlock had publicity cards made up for the Hayden brothers. "When we developed our first press kits, their response to the question of their racing goal was 'to race in the GPs and become world champion,' Sherlock says. "There was no doubt in my mind of their future success. I'm very proud to have been a part of their lives and to have seen their dreams come true." (Cliff Sherlock collection)

CHAPTER 4 THE TRANSITION

It was a Sunday morning, June 30, 1990, and Earl was checking the Haydens out of their Lima, Ohio, hotel room when he saw Scott Parker at the front desk. On Saturday, the family had watched the Michigan racer ride to victory at the Lima half-mile, taking a step toward his third of what would eventually be nine AMA Grand National Championships. Earl had to get the kids to the track for their amateur race, but as usual in such cases, he took time to walk up and shake the factory Harley-Davidson rider's hand. The opportunity for priceless advice on his kids' racing careers was just too good to pass up.

The Haydens relished opportunities to see their heroes in action. They followed the pro circuit by reading magazines and watching race coverage and *Moto World* on television, but attending events in person was obviously the best. These were the men, after all—successors to the legends in the lyrics on Earl's *Motorcycle Man* record—whom the Haydens hoped one day to emulate.

Roger's hero was Ronnie Jones, whose T-shirts he would wear to the races and whose stickers he would plaster on his notebooks. Jones even gave him a number plate at one race, and Earl zip-tied it onto Roger's bicycle.

Tommy didn't play favorites, preferring to like different aspects of different racers, but for Nicky, Bubba Shobert had always been the biggest hero. Riding Hondas, the dirt tracker–turned–road racer had won AMA Grand National dirt track titles in 1985, '86, and '87, then won the AMA Superbike crown in 1988. The following year, while racing in the USGP at Laguna Seca, Shobert had been tragically injured in a cool-down-lap collision with Australian Kevin Magee, prematurely ending his racing career.

A Honda fan, Nicky had taken an early liking to Shobert, and he'd watch a tape of a Dave Despain–narrated documentary on the Californian over and over. Nicky's fondness for Shobert was cemented when he was 7, during one of the family's annual trips to the Indy Mile.

Longing for an autograph from his hero, Nicky was thwarted by the

AMA's minimum-age policy for pit entry, and it looked like he would be going home empty-handed. Amazingly, however, he was able to catch the champ's eye from outside the chain-link fence, and Shobert came around and led him into his work area for a photo and a signature. Ever ambitious, Nicky decided to push his luck and ask for a piece of riding gear. "I laugh now when a kid asks me for a couple of helmets or something, but I'm sure I was that same kid in Bubba's line," he says now.

Shobert was in the process of changing out of his riding gear, so he handed Nicky a sweaty, red riding sock. It wasn't exactly a No. 1 plate or a helmet, but Nicky was smitten. He saved the prize for years, even wearing it in races for a while ("I thought I was pretty cool," he remembers). Shobert himself doesn't recall the incident—just making the day for another kid, as Nicky now does at his races—but he does remember noticing the Hayden family way back during his amateur days, at a race in Ross Downs, near Dallas. "I also remember seeing Earl and the boys in the crowd when I was on the podium at the Springfield Mile one year," he says. "I could see that racing was really exciting to them."

Back in the lobby of that Lima hotel, after congratulating Parker on his victory, Earl got down to business. He explained that Tommy, Nicky, and Roger were 11, 8, and 7, and without hyperbole, he described how they had done so far. "Do you have any advice?" Earl asked. "Do you figure they might have a shot at a career?"

Parker hesitated a moment before answering: "Do you really want to know what I think?" he asked. Earl indicated that he did. "Hey, dirt track's great and it's fun, but for the long-term package, there's not a lot of money there," Parker explained pragmatically. "You're risking your butt out there week in and week out, and road racing has more avenues for making money. I'm not trying to send you out of dirt track, but

if I had a kid in it, I'd have him going where he can make the most money, the easiest, in the shortest amount of time—and that's in road racing."

Parker went on to point out how the GNC tour only supported two full-time factory riders—maximum three—and that the rest of the racers were struggling to make ends meet. The odds of all three Hayden boys landing good positions were less than slim.

This wasn't really news, but coming from Parker, the facts hit home for Earl: Perhaps because of dirt track's resistance to change, the sport was at risk of becoming something of an anachronism. Meanwhile, on the Grand Prix road racing circuit, Americans Kenny Roberts, Freddie Spencer, and Eddie Lawson had won 10 World Championships between them in the last 12 years. That very summer, Wayne Rainey was on his way to his first of three 500cc Grand Prix titles, and John Kocinski was headed to the 250cc world crown. In addition to their nationality, these riders shared something else in common: All had spent their youths sliding around the very same dirt ovals that the Hayden boys were now riding, then found success on the AMA road race circuit before heading overseas.

Obviously, this fact wasn't due to some strange coincidence: Once he has become comfortable—through countless laps—with pitching out the back end on a dirt track bike, a rider isn't liable to mind when a powerful road race machine gets a little loose. "When you start sliding [on the asphalt], you don't start getting spooked," Parker explains. "The dirt tracking experience gives you a hell of an edge in your road racing package."

In the formative years of AMA competition, dirt track and road racing were linked in ways that are difficult to imagine today. (Some dirt trackers still resent the success that has since been enjoyed by their counterparts.) In American motorcycle

RIGHT: Although the Haydens became focused mostly on road racing in the early '90s, they did continue to hit the occasional dirt track, as Tommy shows in 1992 with this slide on his Woods Rotax 600. (Flat Trak Fotos)

ABOVE: Tommy (middle) leaves the start in his very first road race, a CMRA event in Oak Hill, Texas, on the family's sole Yamaha YSR50. "That was a big deal," Tommy remembers. "I finished the race, and the next week we were back with a couple more YSRs, so Nicky could race." (Hayden collection) LEFT: Nicky, Recil Hart, Tommy, and Earl (giving rabbit ears) show off their trio of YSRs at a CMRA race in Texas. Note the leathers for sale in the back of the box van. (Hayden collection)

Earl poses with Nicky and Tommy for a Moto Liberty promotional photo in 1992. Note that Nicky is wearing hand-me-down leathers with Tommy's name still on them. (John Flory/Cliff Sherlock Collection)

racing's early days, the National Champion was decided in a single race—the Springfield Mile—but a series format was introduced in 1954. The series included both dirt track and road race venues; champions were declared in each specialty, but to win the overall championship—the Grand National Championship—one had to be strong on both surfaces. Only in 1976 did the AMA start splitting dirt track and road racing into two separate series, and while road racing had grown in popularity, dirt track had begun to suffer of late. The writing on the wall was clear.

Actually, the Haydens had always known that they eventually wanted to go road racing; that's what Roberts, Shobert, and other heroes had done, so they figured it would happen someday. Tommy still had the Yamaha YSR50 mini road racer that he'd gotten for a birthday (the same one with which they'd raced their imaginary Suzuka 8 Hours), and they'd take it out and ride it in the driveway now and then.

Still, Parker's advice was the impetus Earl needed to start the transition sooner rather than later. Shortly after their talk in Lima, Earl did some checking around and learned about a YSR racing series that was held in Texas under the sanction of the CMRA, a big road racing club. It didn't take him long to act. "That was like on a Monday that he called to find out what it was all about," Tommy says, "and by Friday, we were headed down there to Oak Hill."

Nicky came along as well, but with just one YSR, it was up to big brother to dip his toe in the waters of road racing. Tommy took part in the club's mandatory racing school and then signed up for his first race the same weekend. There was a big field, consisting primarily of adults, and Tommy was the youngest racer. The conditions were rainy, but Tommy ended up finishing pretty well. That was all it took; the Haydens were hooked: "Once we got home, we started selling dirt trackers and buying road racers," Nicky says.

Armed with another YSR, the family headed back to Texas for a race on a kart track the very next week, and this time Nicky raced as well. The Hayden boys' dirt track experience had given them an advantage on other beginning road racers since they weren't intimidated, though they still had plenty with which to familiarize themselves. "Going fast came easy to us, but we wouldn't stick our knees out," Nicky explains, "and it took a bit of work to start using the front brake."

In addition, the Haydens' racing lines weren't ideal, and Earl heard it from some of their competitors for the brothers' habit of going up the inside into corners. (In dirt track, you never let someone get away with leaving the door open.)

Those had been the final two CMRA races of the season, but during the winter, Earl picked up another YSR50 and also bought a Honda RS125. When springtime hit, the Haydens made their traditional trip to Daytona for the amateur dirt track races, but by now they were primarily focused on road racing. As the first CMRA race of 1991 approached, the Hayden brothers rode their bicycles down to Kuester's Hardware in Owensboro and bought some industrial-strength Velcro, which they attached to the knees of their dirt track leathers with Super Glue. This way, they could attach the plastic pucks that road racers wear for protection as they drag their knees on the ground around corners. It wasn't long until they were putting those knee sliders to good use.

That summer, the Hayden boys made numerous trips out to Texas for the YSR races, either with Earl or with Recil, learning the art of road racing. Club rules were that beginning riders had to wear yellow shirts until they could make it through two races without crashing, but Nicky was having trouble making it that far. "Eventually, my shirt got so ripped up that I just had to throw it away," he says. "Fortunately, they let it slide."

The Haydens improved quickly, and it didn't take them

long to pick up sponsorship from Sam Yamashita's Moto Liberty, a Dallas shop that was seriously into road racing. "Those guys didn't care—they just turned the throttle and went," recalls Danny Walker, who worked and raced with Moto Liberty at the time. "Nicky would run the thing until it ran out of gas."

In '92, the shop brought in two Honda RS125s for the Haydens to try out. The brothers were so small that they could barely fit on the bikes, and the fuel tank on one even had to be reshaped so that Roger could reach the handlebars. Nonetheless, the brothers began racing the 125s (along with the 50s) in CMRA events.

"Tommy would set a certain speed and stay there until Nicky beat him," Walker says. "Once that happened, he'd take a step. Nicky would push him out of his comfort zone."

It was while they were riding for Moto Liberty that the Hayden family hooked up with Bruce Porter, who oversees Arai helmets' U.S. racing program. The team had invited Earl, Tommy, and Nicky to attend an AMA banquet in California, where their adult riders would be presented with an award. Although the Haydens themselves weren't up for any prizes, Earl knew the room would be filled with industry heavy-hitters, so he wanted to make an impression. In Porter's case, at least, he succeeded.

"The lights were dimmed as the show was about to fire up, and the emcee walked out," Porter remembers. "Everyone was focused on the stage, and right at that moment, as if it were perfectly choreographed, the doors in the back of the room swung open, and the light from the sun came through. In walked Earl Hayden, and behind Earl were two little boys wearing black tuxedos with tails and top hats. The building hushed, and everyone watched them walk all the way to the front and take their seats. I thought, 'You know, here's a show-man. There's something special here.'"

The next morning, Porter introduced himself to Earl at breakfast, told him he'd followed the family's progress, and said he would love the opportunity to work together. All three Haydens have worn Arai helmets ever since.

It was around this time that Nicky vowed to his friend Eric Reynolds that he would be a teetotaler—if not permanently, then at least for a long while. "I'd see these kids who were older than me drinking at the Amateur Nationals and then doing terrible the next day," Nicky says. "My plan then was to never drink until I won a world championship."

Soon, Earl began signing Tommy up to race the RS125 in full-size races—mainly the 125cc class at WERA regional club races. Perhaps the top road racing club in the country, WERA also represented somewhat of a break for the Haydens, as most of the venues it visited—Putnam Park near Indianapolis, Gateway International Raceway in St. Louis, Ohio's Nelson Ledges, Michigan's Grattan Raceway—were relatively close to Owensboro.

That said, the Haydens also missed the idyllic old days of traveling the country together as a family. Nicky and Roger weren't initially ready for WERA racing (even with Nicky's fudged AMA card), so for a while anyway, the family found itself splitting up on weekends. And whereas the Hayden

ABOVE: Danny Walker shows the Haydens his Moto Liberty Yamaha 250, along with his teammate Doug Carmichael (red hat). The brothers rode for the shop as well, and years later, they would help Walker at his American Supercamp riding schools. (Hayden collection)

brothers had always taken their racing seriously, their efforts took on more urgency as they got up to speed in road racing.

And get up to speed they did. Tommy caught on quickly and soon began posting some good results on the white Honda RS125. The boys were about average in size for their ages, but they were now riding essentially full-size bikes, and announcers took to calling Tommy the "Flyin' Flea." Clad in dirt track leathers, he enjoyed a good power-to-weight advantage over much of his competition, and his racing instincts had been well-honed in dirt track. Since he hadn't yet accumulated many points, he had to start from the backs of the grids with the novices, but he routinely slashed his way through the pack to the experts.

Compared to dirt track, where riders must spend a lot of time in the pits while track maintenance is performed, the Haydens enjoyed the extra seat time they were getting in road racing. "I've always liked to ride, and it was nice getting to ride a lot," Nicky says.

By now, Tommy and Nicky had pretty much adapted, and although they still had a few hold-over bad habits from dirt track, their past experience had mainly served them well. The brothers were quickly developing a reputation, and they began receiving help from sponsors from Texas shops—first Moto Liberty and later Southwest Motorsports.

At the time, American Honda parts manager Brian Uchida was in charge of selling parts to people who had RS125s and 250s in the country. "[The Haydens] would order stuff from me, but I was hearing from everybody else how these kids were going to be really good," says Uchida, who finally saw for himself how good they were when the Haydens competed in Southern California at Willow Springs International Raceway.

At first, Earl would order parts from Uchida, but after a while, the father handed that responsibility over to Tommy. "The poor kid was so timid," Uchida says with a laugh. "You could tell it was really hard for him, but of course I was pretty easy on him. I could tell from him and his dad that they were a really good family."

At that season's year-end Grand National Finals—a huge amateur event attended by factory-team bosses looking for a peek at the future—Tommy became the youngest-ever WERA race winner.

The feat got considerable press and put Tommy on the map, and in '93, he and Nicky began racing WERA's National Series—a step below the AMA tour. A Yamaha TZR250 was added to the Haydens' stable, and the two brothers started campaigning WERA's National Endurance Series (longer races run under a multirider team format). The travel schedule picked up again, with trips out to Miami, Seattle, and Willow Springs, and Tommy and Nicky finished 1-2 in the 125cc class that season.

Roger was starting to get in the mix as well, riding YSRs at age 11 and 125s when he turned 12. (Like his older brothers, he had some bad habits at first, even putting his foot down in corners from time to time!) The family was reunited in a way, with all three brothers once again going to the same races on the same weekends.

Tommy turned 15 in July 1993, but according to his AMA license, he was 16. That made him eligible for his Pro-Am classification and to begin racing as a pro in some AMA dirt track events (though not in Grand Nationals). Tommy started hitting Pro-Am races around the Midwest, accumulating points so he could advance to the Expert level. One of the races Tommy entered was the first amateur Mile ever held at the Indianapolis State Fairgrounds. "Here the kid was underage, and he walked away with the Pro-Am class!" says Ken Saillant, who promoted the race.

On August 8 of that year, Tommy entered his first professional AMA road race at Mid-Ohio Sports Car Course in the

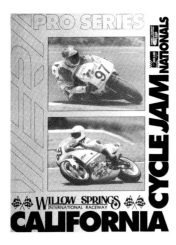

250cc GP class. (AMA Pro Racing has an age minimum of 16 years, which 15-year-old Tommy was able to circumvent thanks to Earl having fudged his age years before.) Now defunct, the 250 GP class was the AMA's entry class into professional racing, but it was also the domain of several established veterans, including Danny Walker and class ruler Rich Oliver. Oliver had heard about the Haydens from their WERA exploits, but this was his first time getting to see one of them in action.

"I remember two things," Oliver recalls of Tommy. "One was that he was wearing these big glasses, and the other was that he was really good. Everyone was watching him because he was so young and so new, and he was so small that he could barely get on the bike, but he wasn't afraid to go fast in the corners."

As their exploits continued to pile up, the Hayden boys were beginning to draw some attention, regularly appearing in *Cycle News* and earning a reputation in the paddock as young racers with a strong future. Earl felt the time was right for putting them on the radar of some of the factory teams. Already, he had made a point of mentioning them in his talks with fast riders like Parker and Oliver, whose knowledge and contacts he valued. "He was always cool about it," Oliver remembers. "He's a racer dad, but he's not overly pushy. He just lets their talent speak for itself, and that's the best way."

Earl knew that promotion was a part of the game, but he also recognized that there wasn't a shortage of parents with a high opinion of their kids. "I didn't want to talk them up too much, because that's what you'd expect a parent to do," Earl says. "I just wanted to plant a seed early. I'd talk to the managers on the factory teams, and I'd say, 'Remember me in seven years.' Eventually, though, I knew we needed somebody besides Daddy telling people these kids were good."

Earl decided that what his boys needed was a business manager, and as usual, he didn't think small. Through his company International Racers, Inc., Gary Howard represented most of the top American Grand Prix racers—Kenny Roberts, Eddie Lawson, Wayne Rainey among them—and despite his kids' relative inexperience, that's where Earl decided to start. He approached Howard, and the agent agreed to visit the Haydens in Owensboro for a meeting. He was impressed with what he saw and heard, and his agency began an unofficial relationship with the Haydens in early 1994.

Having Howard in their corner was obviously helpful in terms of representation, but perhaps more valuable was the access to knowledge that the arrangement afforded. Gary asked another of his riders, Jimmy Filice, to keep an eye on the Haydens at the races and to help them develop, just as he had already done with Kenny Roberts' sons, Kenny Jr. and Kurtis. Filice was a talented AMA dirt tracker and road racer (and occasional Grand Prix wild-card entrant), and he had dominated the '93 AMA 250cc GP series while riding an Otsuka Electronics–sponsored Yamaha for a team owned by Rainey.

Tommy accompanied Filice to the first AMA race of the '94 season in Daytona. Nicky was busy racing at the dirt track a couple of miles down International Speedway Boulevard, but Tommy's job was to forego riding in favor of shadowing Filice, observing firsthand the process a top rider followed at an important race. "We'd get up every morning and go to the racetrack and work," Filice recalls. "He'd just see how things were done, how I worked with the mechanic—just see how I approached the weekend."

When Filice won Daytona's 250cc race, it had been a valuable lesson indeed.

Nicky (69) leads Tommy during the 1993 WERA Grand National Finals at Road Atlanta. "They just had natural talent from the beginning," says WERA president Evelyne Clark. "They were unbeatable, but they were also polite and a pleasure to deal with. I'm so proud that they got their start in road racing with us." (Hayden collection)

CHAPTER 5

GOING INTERNATIONAL

Tommy in action at Jerez: "The Ducados series was really strong at the time," he says. "We were in over our heads a little, but it showed us how many levels there still were above us. We went home and got to work." (Carlos Rufas)

FAR LEFT: While his brothers got road racing experience, Roger Lee, shown here proudly sitting on a Hart Racing YZ80 with a low pipe, continued his dirt track efforts. Note the trimmed-down seat. (Hayden collection)

LEFT: Nicky (33) dices in the pack in Jerez, Spain, during the Open Ducados. Loaded with talented riders, the race was a wake-up call—and not just because Nicky crashed and knocked himself out. (Carlos Rufas)

ABOVE: In the garage at the Open Ducados, Nicky tells Tommy where he likes his front brake lever positioned while the adults watch on with interest. (Hayden collection)

The billboards were the first tip-off that the Haydens were entering a completely foreign realm—and it wasn't just the fact that the writing was in Spanish. Earl, Tommy, and Nicky had just disembarked in Jerez, and despite the fact that they were in Spain, the cigarette advertisements all featured American motorcycle racers—Wayne Rainey for Marlboro, Kevin Schwantz for Lucky Strike. With the jet lag, it took a few minutes to sink in, but for a family involved in a fringe sport that few from the mainstream understood or even knew about, seeing their "unknown" heroes' likenesses on display in an airport terminal was a shock.

It was 1994, and though Spain had a thriving economy, it no longer enjoyed the world power status it did in prior centuries. In terms of motorcycle racing, however, the country was and is the world capital. Because youngsters can ride scooters on public streets, and because bikes are easy to maneuver and park in the cramped villages, motorcycling is an integral part of Spain's culture. The country was already home to great tracks like Jerez de la Frontera, Circuit de Catalunya, and Circuito del Jarama—all of which had hosted Grand Prix rounds the previous year, and the World Championship Road Race Series was even headquartered in Spain, as Madrid company Dorna had taken over the championship's commercial and TV rights just two years earlier.

Such was Spain's infatuation with motorcycle racing that it couldn't be sated by multiple annual Grand Prix races. The country's strongest national series—the Open Ducados, named after the tobacco company that sponsored it—offered big enough prize purses, had good enough TV coverage, and attracted big enough crowds and fast enough riders, that it was arguably more prestigious than the European championship. Spanish aces like Luis D'Antin, Jorge Martinez Aspar, Sete Gibernau, and Carlos Checa had taken part, and since it was also open to foreigners, racers like American Kenny Roberts Jr. had also competed. Now, with very limited road racing experience, Tommy and Nicky would be making a two-race appearance in the Open Ducados.

"I was pretty young, and I didn't really know exactly what I was

getting into," Nicky remembers. "I saw Schwantz and Rainey on those billboards, and I was thinking, 'Man, this is the real deal over here!'"

At just 15 and 12, Tommy and Nicky were indeed young, though back home, the AMA assumed them to be 16 and 14. AMA rules stipulate that a rider must be at least 4 years old to race, and Earl—whose brother owned a printing company—had doctored Tommy and Nicky's birth certificates (the former by one year, the latter by two) to get them racing when they were just young boys.

Despite the boys' small sizes, carrying off the ruse hadn't been especially difficult—in part because they were always so fast. Even when Nicky was racing in the 7-11 class at the Amateur Nationals for the first time, he was competitive enough that bystanders just scratched their heads and shrugged, assuming he must be the world's smallest 7-year-old.

The Haydens just wanted to race, and they avoided the issue as much as possible, even within the family. When report-

ers would bring it up, Earl would say vaguely that he preferred to leave their ages out of stories. "You'd ask those kids their age, and they'd get scared because they couldn't remember how old they were supposed to be!" Larry Pegram says with a laugh.

If anyone had checked closely enough, they'd have seen that the whole time the Hayden kids were growing up, Jenny and Nicky were only five and a half months apart on their AMA cards—a physical impossibility! "Jenny was second, and then all of a sudden Nicky was older than Jenny," Pegram remembers. "I was like, 'Hey, how'd that happen?' It was just kind of for chuckles. I don't think anybody knew exactly how old they were, but we all knew there was something funny."

There was also the issue of school levels. In general the Haydens endeavored to be vague about that subject, but when Nicky was pinned down, he would say that he had been held back because of his dyslexia. (He really *had* been forced to repeat a grade once, so he had to say he'd been held back twice.)

As the Hayden brothers grew older and faster, earning reputations as talented racers, the age discrepancy started to become less of a concern for the family. Not only were they winning against the older kids in their classes, but when young pros like Pegram or Scott Stump would drop by Owensboro and practice at Sunset Downs, the kids could actually hang with them on their home track. "That kind of gave them some confidence," Earl says.

Still, the issue did pop up every now and then. Two-time Grand National Champion Gary Nixon remembers hanging out once at the Lima Half-Mile, watching the racing from the Haydens' van, when out of the blue, he asked Nicky his age. "In this high-pitched voice, he says, 'Um, 15?'" Nixon says. "I laughed and went, 'Oh yeah?' He looked like he was about 12 or something."

BELOW: Having washed the Haydens' collection of bikes in front of the family garage, Nicky grabs a ball and bat in preparation for some summer fun. (Hayden collection)

LEFT: With a pillow prop to help his feet reach the pedals, a 12-year-old Nicky takes the box van wheel for a spell during a cross-country trip to California for a race at Willow Springs in 1993. (Hayden collection)

Nicky gets some early champagne-spraying experience at Texas World Speedway after winning a sprint race in the mid-90s. The drive from Owensboro was nearly 1,000 miles, and Oak Hill was about 750 miles, but the Haydens made trips to Texas on a regular basis. (Hayden collection)

Despite road racing's popularity in Spain, the country's Grand Prix success had thus far been limited to small-displacement specialists like Sito Pons and Angel Nieto. Americans, meanwhile, had dominated the premier class, with Schwantz, Rainey, Eddie Lawson, Freddie Spencer, and Kenny Roberts Sr. having taken thirteen of the last sixteen 500cc titles. Roberts, Rainey, and Randy Mamola all had places near Barcelona in a town called Sitges, and they were revered by the Spanish fans.

"As an American, you need some sort of a base where you can drop your hat," Mamola says. "Sitges is right on the beach, it has nice weather, and it's a nice town with great food. Also, it's only 25 minutes from one of the nicest cities in Europe, and it's just 20 minutes from the airport."

Just one year earlier, while defending his third World Championship, Rainey had suffered paralyzing injuries in a crash at the Misano Grand Prix in Italy. Unable to pull himself away from motorcycle racing, he had already taken over Roberts' Yamaha-mounted, Marlboro-backed 250cc GP team, with Gibernau and Junior as riders. In addition, the Open Ducados organizers had made it clear that they'd help Rainey if he wanted to field riders in their series.

As luck would have it, Gary Howard—on the lookout for unique opportunities for his newest, youngest clients—had also approached Rainey about just such a possibility. "It was real early in my recovery," Rainey says, "and there was a lot of interest at that time. There were some easy opportunities that were available to me."

Rainey had met the Haydens once when they had visited his home in Monterey, California, but he had never seen them ride. Nonetheless, after lining up some TZs from Yamaha and borrowing a couple of mechanics from his GP team, he arranged for Jimmy Filice and the two oldest Hayden brothers

to compete in the Open Ducados' Jerez and Jarama rounds, which were on back-to-back weekends.

The American contingent, including the Roberts and Rainey teams, would spend much of the time hanging out together. Filice, who was entered in the 250cc class, came straight to Spain from Austria, where he had substituted for an injured Kenny Roberts Jr. on Rainey's 250cc GP team. Kurtis Roberts—Junior's younger brother—would be racing the 125cc class, along with Tommy and Nicky.

The Haydens arrived on Wednesday and after a night's sleep in their hotel, headed to the Jerez circuit, which had hosted a Grand Prix just a few weeks earlier. "I remember being out there walking around the track, thinking about how the GP had just been there," Nicky says. "It was definitely going to be the first time I rode on a real GP track."

Although they had by now backed off on their dirt track schedule and were focusing almost exclusively on road racing, Tommy and Nicky still lacked considerable asphalt experience, and what they did have had come on a different bike—the Honda RS125. This was also the Haydens' first time overseas (even for Earl), and they were coming over in the middle of a series in which the competition had already had a few races to get up to speed. The track was much faster than anything they'd ever ridden, and of course there was the age issue.

While applying for passports for the trip, Earl had realized they might have a problem. Examination of the fine print revealed that there would be stiff fines for falsifying information, so Earl consulted Gary Howard. Together, they decided to fill out the paperwork with the boys' true ages.

When he was questioned by Filice, Earl admitted that the boys were actually 15 and 12. Eventually, Wayne Rainey approached him about it. "It was kind of a big issue, with pressure put on everybody," Rainey says. "I could see it wasn't a comfortable situation, but it wasn't as much of an issue for me as it was for Earl."

Rainey decided to look the other way, and the team did what they could to get the brothers on the pace. Nicky could barely reach the ground, and the mechanics had to bend in his front brake lever so his fingers could reach it. That the kids were being thrown in at the deep end became immediately apparent in practice.

"Every session, the officials would bring back in four or five pickup-truck loads of crashed bikes," Earl says. "I thought, 'Man, is *this* what it's going to be like?' That really stuck in my mind—'Are these kids going to have to ride like *this* to be competitive?' That was an eye-opener."

It was an eye-opener for Rainey as well. Tommy at least had proper technique, but Nicky was still riding like a dirt tracker, surprising riders behind him by downshifting far too early. "They were just kids—young boys," Rainey says. "We brought them over, and when we watched them go around the circuit, I wasn't quite sure if we were doing the right thing at the time, to tell you the truth. I knew at that stage we had our hands full."

Unfortunately, Rainey wasn't able to spend much time coaching the kids. The Spanish people—not just fans and media, but even officials—still hadn't come to terms with the fact that their invincible hero was in a wheelchair, and Rainey was bombarded by emotional well-wishers. His time was limited, and about all he could tell Tommy and Nicky was to have fun, that this wasn't a high-pressure tryout.

The 36-rider grid was huge compared to what the Haydens were used to, but even more daunting was the 60-rider field that was trying to qualify. Amazingly, Tommy and Nicky somehow made it into the main event, but Nicky's race didn't last long. As the pack roared into the first turn, he and another rider touched, and Nicky crashed hard.

"I remember he was just spinning sideways, off the bike, flying through the air, right through the middle of that whole pack," Rainey says. "I was just praying that he was okay; I didn't need this already."

"I hit my head pretty good, and I didn't remember anything when I got up," Nicky says. "I'd been knocked out a bunch, but it was the first time I ever woke up and people were talking to me in Spanish. I was lost."

The rest of the event was typical 125cc racing—close and intense—and Tommy survived to finish mid pack. Meanwhile, Filice topped the 250cc race, and that night, the group showed the Haydens how professionals celebrate a race win.

Nicky struggled in his first overseas race at Jerez, but he learned a lot. Little did he know that 12 years later, he would be back at the track, standing on the MotoGP podium. (Carlos Rufas)

The dinner was boisterous to say the least, and the shenanigans carried over into the hotel.

"They were acting pretty wild," Nicky says. "I remember somebody broke out a fire extinguisher and sprayed it under somebody's door. It covered everything in the room! I was like, 'God, these guys are *wild*!'"

With their trial by fire in Jerez under their belts, the Haydens felt a bit better going into the Jarama round the next weekend. At least they knew what they were in for, and they were a bit closer to being on the pace. Tommy qualified 12th, but in the race, it was his turn to crash in turn 1; he was taken out in a five-bike pileup, while Nicky made it to the finish in mid pack.

"I don't think we were really prepared to just go do a two-race stint like that," Tommy admits. "Looking back, I know how things need to be. You can't show up at a race at a new track with a new team and have very high expectations. You're putting yourself in a deep hole to start with, but you don't always have the opportunities to make everything the way you want it. You have to take advantage of what you have."

Earl had another scare when he went to pick up the boys' prize money. "I got worried to death about them checking the passport and it showing their real age," he says. Fortunately, the passports were only needed as photo identification, and the clerk didn't even check the ages.

Although they hadn't set the world on fire in their introduction to big-time road racing, the Haydens at least knew where they stood, and they knew what they had to work on. They were motivated to improve, but Rainey decided that they weren't yet ready for another whack at the Open Ducados.

"I can't say Wayne just totally turned his back on us, but we weren't at the level he was hoping," Nicky says. "We didn't get invited back, but Wayne was really honest about every-thing, and he gave us a big opportunity there. Even now, Jerez is always kind of a special place for me when we go there for the GP, because I did ride it so early in my career."

Just a few months after Tommy and Nicky's return from Spain, they were treated to another encounter with international road racing, only this time from the perspective of spectators. The occasion was the 1994 United States Grand Prix, at the historic Laguna Seca circuit in Monterey, California. Though it had enjoyed some good years, the race was by now experiencing financial troubles, and Dorna had stepped in to promote it. It was clear that this would be the last USGP for some time—perhaps ever. But for Tommy and Nicky, who had never even been to an AMA road race, it was still a big deal.

Their attendance had been made possible by Redline Oil's Cliff Sherlock, a sponsor who wanted his young riders to see a real Grand Prix and perhaps make some connections that would prove useful some day. The boys flew out to California by themselves, and Sherlock and his wife picked them up and brought them to the track. Gary Howard had arranged for credentials, but the Haydens were still too young to be allowed in the paddock. Taking matters into their own hands, they squeezed under the chain-link fence and roamed the pits, in awe at the incredible level of professionalism on display. "I remember standing outside the interview room and seeing Max Biaggi there in his Dainese Aprilia leathers," recalls Nicky of the Italian ace, who was on his way to winning his first 250cc World Championship that year.

In the end, it wasn't exactly an all-American affair, with Italians Luca Cadalora and Doriano Romboni winning the 500cc and 250cc classes, respectively, and Japanese rider Takeshi Tsujimura topping the 125cc race. Nonetheless, Laguna had left its mark on the Hayden brothers.

A faxed copy of the August 15, 1994, AMA Pro Racing press release announcing the suspension of Tommy for falsifying his age: "The risk and liability exposure created by such an action for the AMA, race promoters and other competitors is enormous," Competition Director Merrill Vanderslice was quoted as saying. (Hayden collection)

Earl felt butterflies in his stomach as he walked into the AMA offices with Tommy and Nicky's birth certificates in a folder tucked under his arm. Following the experience of the Open Ducados, it had been clear to Earl that the stakes had changed on the age issue, and he knew he would have to address it. Earl and Gary Howard agreed that it was best to come forward with the information, let the chips fall where they may, and get it all over with.

After the Amateur Nationals in July 1994, Earl had called the AMA to schedule a meeting with Hugh Fleming. Fleming, who was in charge of amateur racing, was curious about why it was necessary to meet in person, but Earl insisted on making the five-hour drive northeast to Westerville.

What the Haydens had done with their ages wasn't completely unheard of. Many other big-name racers had fudged their birthdays, especially back in the old days (though few are willing to go on the record about it, even now). Besides, in the Haydens' eyes, what they were doing was relatively harmless. By passing for *older* than their real ages, Tommy and Nicky were actually making things more difficult for themselves. "It's a lot different than if a kid's lying and saying he's younger —riding the Mini Jr. class when he should be in the Mini Sr. class or something like that," Larry Pegram insists.

Unfortunately, the AMA didn't see it that way. After Earl presented his information to Fleming and a couple of other staffers, the penalty was handed down, and Tommy got the worst of it. He had been accumulating Pro-Am points in order to earn his Expert license, which—when he had earned enough points there—would eventually enable him to get a provisional GNC license and start racing in Grand National TT and Short Track events (but not Half-Miles and Miles). Following the meeting, though, the AMA threw out all of the Pro-Am points

he had earned up to that time, and he was suspended from AMA competition for one year. Because Nicky hadn't yet received his Pro-Am license, his sanction was a simple six-month ban.

At Earl's request, the AMA agreed to give the Haydens some time to speak with their sponsors before an announcement was made, but word was leaked almost immediately. In addition, no effort was made to explain that the Haydens had come forward voluntarily, so some people assumed the boys had been caught and accused the family of cheating. This made Earl feel bad for his kids, since the fudging of their ages had been his decision.

Still, the consequences could have been worse. Most of the other racers didn't make a big deal out of it, and the Haydens didn't lose any friends over the issue. Since it was already toward the end of the season, the timing of the suspension was fortuitous, and in the meantime, the kids could still compete in WERA events and outlaw races. "It slowed us down a little bit, but it wasn't that big a deal," Tommy recalls.

In a way, the suspension was almost a blessing in disguise. It gave the Hayden family a bit of a break, both financially and logistically, and it taught them a lesson about sensitive information and how people you don't even know can make assumptions.

The bottom line, however, was that the Haydens were okay with their own actions. They weren't proud of what they had done, but neither were they ashamed. Running with older kids had allowed them to improve at a faster rate without hurting anyone, and when it had become clear that the ruse was

no longer quite so innocent, they had been honest and then accepted responsibility for their actions.

"I think Earl wanted to make the situation right, and he did," Wayne Rainey says. "With an opportunity like that, if my kid was racing, I don't know if I wouldn't have done the same thing."

When Tommy really did turn 16, in July 1994, he went down to the Kentucky Department of Motor Vehicles and got his driver's license. Soon, he was taking Nicky and Roger to outlaw races at indoor dirt tracks, where they would make a little money competing against older riders. When Earl couldn't go on these trips, he would tell the boys he wouldn't pay for their entry fees unless they could find someone to film the races so that he could watch them when they got home. Eric Reynolds was often brought along as the Haydens' official cameraman. "I didn't like that job too much," Reynolds says. "One time Earl paid me $69 to film at the Amateur Nationals, and that just lasted a few minutes before I was off running around somewhere. We got home, and he wanted to know where the tape was."

Once, the brothers took off in the middle of a snowstorm for a race in Cleveland, Tommy driving the entire 450 miles at 40 mph. Often, they'd go straight from a dirt track to a road race, with Rose sometimes meeting them on the road in between to swap machinery between vans.

On one occasion, the brothers even traveled to California without a chaperone. They hit snow in Colorado, by which time Tommy had been driving the van for about 20 hours straight, and when he said he had to pull over for a nap, Nicky—long before having earned his permit—volunteered to take the wheel for a while. "He pulls out of the gas station and onto the on- ramp, and spins a doughnut!" Tommy remembers. "We hadn't even got on the highway yet. I said, 'All right, you're done.' "

In September 1996, Tommy found himself back in Spain—this time on a dirt track bike. The year after the Haydens' Open Ducados adventure, Roberts had opened his Kenny Roberts Training Camp (KRTC), an academy that catered to up-and-coming European and Asian racers who were eager to utilize the mysterious American art of dirt track to improve their road racing skills. Filice and Mamola were instructors, and Roberts had a fleet of Honda XR100 minibikes that the students would ride on a small dirt oval at the Barcelona Olympic facility.

To promote the camp and dirt track racing in general, Roberts decided to put on an exhibition dirt track race in Barcelona, and he brought over several American celebrity racers to take part. The first year, he had invited Filice and Eddie Lawson, as well as dirt trackers Steve Morehead and Ronnie Jones. In '96, Tommy got the invite, along with Jones and dirt track legend Jay Springsteen. Filice and Mamola would also compete. Called Marlboro Dirt Track USA, the event was held in conjunction with the popular Catalunya Grand Prix (the 13th stop on that season's GP tour), and admission was free.

Now 17, Tommy was much more mature than he'd been on his last trip to Spain, and he even had some GNC racing under his belt. He and Nicky had planned to come back over in 1995, but the two collided while training with just a few days to go. Nicky had broken his ankle, and the trip had been called off. Nicky wasn't invited on this particular junket, but Tommy was hungry to show what he had.

Still, for someone who had yet to win a National, he was once again in some pretty lofty company. Filice had topped the previous year's exhibition race, and Mamola had only recently retired from Grand Prix racing after finishing a close second in the title chase on several occasions. Jones was a 10-time AMA Grand National race winner, and Springsteen was a veritable god, with three AMA Grand National Championships to his credit. Even King Kenny himself—AMA Grand National Champion in '73 and '74—would be putting in a few laps. In addition, racing great Dick Mann and Ken Maely were invited along as special guests.

"Those guys were my heroes growing up," Tommy says. "Hanging out with Springer and those guys was the coolest thing, although looking back at it, [the dirt track race] was kind of small-picture compared to everything else that was going on over there."

The exhibition event was held on the Friday and Saturday prior to the Grand Prix, and during a break in GP qualifying, the dirt track contingent suited up and did a parade lap around the famous road race circuit on their Rotaxes. On Saturday night, all of the Grand Prix racers were presented to the sizeable crowd, and they did a lap of honor around the dirt track on their scooters.

Apart from the American contingent, most of the racers in the exhibition were Spanish and Italian. The European riders weren't really in the same league as the Americans, but the spectators were excited, because this was an opportunity to not only see several legends in action, but also to get a rare firsthand taste of the grassroots racing genre that had made the Americans so dominant in Grand Prix racing.

Despite its foreign locale, the $3/8$-Mile track was certainly worthy of riders like Springsteen and Roberts, as it had been painstakingly prepared by Filice in the week leading up to the race. "The track was one of the best tracks I've ever ridden, to this day," Tommy recalls. "It was really, really fun to ride. It was wide and perfectly smooth. You could ride anywhere on it, and it was real easy to pass."

Friday's race was really a glorified warm-up, and Filice had taken the win. On Saturday, the qualifying format featured numerous heat races in order to give the packed house as good a show as possible. Tommy faced Filice in his heat, and impressively, the youngster pulled off the win.

"He kind of surprised me," Filice admits. "It was like my home territory. I was running the school and I prepared the track, so I was pretty confident of doing well. Tommy beat my butt."

The youngster's qualifying times were as good as anyone's, and he definitely had the attention of his famous competitors. "He was very young at that point, but he was already a very good rider," Roberts recalls. "He had good style for a dirt tracker."

In the main, Tommy came off the start line with Springsteen, and the two put on a crowd-pleasing battle throughout the race.

"We raced back and forth, and it came right down to the last lap," says Springsteen, who was 39 at the time, and who eventually took the victory. Tommy was a close runner-up over Jones and Filice, impressing everyone in attendance and somewhat vindicating his earlier Open Ducados experience.

"It was good for me because when I went over there the first time, I didn't have a lot of experience road racing," Tommy says. "I definitely had a long way to go. With flat track, I'd been doing it a long time, and I was a lot more competitive. It was good just meeting and talking to people, and getting some recognition for riding. It was good exposure, and hopefully, the people could see my potential a little bit more."

Tommy in action in one of his first AMA road races at Mid-Ohio Sports Car Course in 1994. As the oldest brother, his job was to get up to speed and learn the scene, then pass on his knowledge to his brothers. (Riles/Nelson)

CHAPTER 6

IN THE SHOW

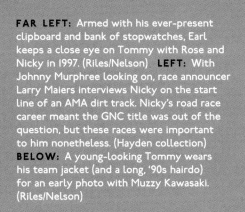

FAR LEFT: Armed with his ever-present clipboard and bank of stopwatches, Earl keeps a close eye on Tommy with Rose and Nicky in 1997. (Riles/Nelson) LEFT: With Johnny Murphree looking on, race announcer Larry Maiers interviews Nicky on the start line of an AMA dirt track. Nicky's road race career meant the GNC title was out of the question, but these races were important to him nonetheless. (Hayden collection) BELOW: A young-looking Tommy wears his team jacket (and a long, '90s hairdo) for an early photo with Muzzy Kawasaki. (Riles/Nelson)

OPPOSITE: Tommy heads through a corner while Muzzy teammate Doug Chandler keeps an eye on him from behind. Many people still compare Tommy's smooth style to that of the three-time AMA Superbike champ. (Riles/Nelson)

When the front door slammed and Tommy finally came walking out of the house, Nicky and Roger stopped digging and leaned on their shovels. "That better have been the Pope you were talking to!" Nicky exclaimed, sweat dripping off his nose. "Where the heck have you been?"

Earl had put the boys to work fixing a water leak in the front yard, and the oldest brother had gone inside to take a phone call. By the time he finally emerged from the house a half hour later, Nicky and Roger wanted an explanation.

As it turned out, Tommy had a pretty good excuse. On the phone had been respected team owner and tuner Rob Muzzy, calling to offer Tommy a factory ride in 600cc Supersport (a talent-packed support class for AMA Superbike) for the 1997 season. "It was kind of out of the blue," says Tommy, who had never even spoken to Muzzy before. "He said, 'I'm working on my team for next year, and I'm looking for a young rider. Are you available? Would you be interested?' Obviously, I said yeah."

Tommy had been focusing on dirt track since serving out his penalty in March 1995. That season (at an honest 16), he had competed in the AMA Hot Shoe and Grand National Championship series as a Pro-Am rider, racing for a small team out of Alabama and often traveling alone or without his brothers. He quickly made up the points he had been docked and was advanced to Expert status, and soon he had enough points to get a provisional GNC license and compete in Grand National Short Tracks and TTs. Tommy made his first national at the Peoria TT (with only Rose on hand to share the moment), and in '96—the year of his graduation from high school—he made the main at the season-opening Daytona national in Florida and posted a top-10 finish at the Du Quoin Mile.

Still, Tommy had managed to hit the occasional club road race on off weekends, in addition to a couple of AMA road race nationals, racing in first the 250cc GP class and the 600cc Supersport division. It was Tommy's '96 Mid-Ohio showing that had caught Muzzy's attention. Through the Haydens' involvement with Gary Howard, Muzzy Kawasaki rider Doug Chandler—on his way to his second of three AMA Superbike titles—took some time to tutor Tommy that weekend. The race was run in wet conditions and featured several red flags, and Tommy—running Metzeler tires and comfortable with limited traction—had been one of the top privateers, with a 15th-place finish. It was enough to convince Muzzy, and Tommy found himself on a real professional road race team. "It's what I had always dreamed about," he says.

Meanwhile, Nicky and Roger were still campaigning the amateur ranks. When they accompanied Tommy to that '96 Mid-Ohio race, they weren't even allowed on pit road, so they stood up on the garage balconies with stopwatches. It was apparent that they were still kids; at one point, they got in trouble with security for riding a scooter on some off-limits trails on the circuit's infield (they tried to talk their way out of it, but the mud on the fender was a giveaway). Still, the younger brothers were impressed by their exposure to the "big time."

"It was exciting getting to go in the garages," Nicky remembers. "They weren't just cleaning off the fairings; they were actually doing the suspension and stuff! It was like being at the Super Bowl or something."

Nicky was also growing up away from the racetracks. Earl employed a couple of big guys to handle repossessions when 2nd Chance Auto customers didn't pay their bills, and Nicky would sometimes accompany them on their rounds. "I guess I just liked the risk," he says.

Inspired by Tommy's signing to Muzzy, Nicky applied a professional approach to his amateur endeavors. With 14 amateur championships and five Amateur National titles, he had nothing to prove going into his final Amateur Nationals in Indianapolis. Nevertheless, he dominated the week, winning on the TT course, the Half-Mile, and—despite botching the start and giving up most of a straightaway to the pack—the Mile as well. A disqualification in a heat race was the only flaw

in an otherwise perfect week, and the performance earned Nicky the inaugural Horizon Award, a prestigious prize awarded by the AMA to recognize riders in their various Amateur Nationals , including Motocross, who seem on the verge of successful transitions to professional racing.

Nicky was closing in on his 16th birthday, and he was hopeful of teaming up with Tommy. Muzzy let him take part in a test at Monterey, California's Laguna Seca Raceway early that season. It was the first time Nicky had ever been on a four-stroke road racer, and although he set a respectable pace, he dragged the engine case in the tight last corner at the end of the day and crashed. "The hardest thing for me to learn [in road racing] was to lean off," Nicky says. "It just didn't feel right. That wasn't a problem on a two-stroke because they were so narrow, but four-strokes dragged."

That night, Muzzy told Nicky that he thought he was too aggressive. He said he'd prepare Tommy's old 600 for him, but he'd have to get the bike and himself to the races.

The season had three rounds after his July 30 birthday— Pikes Peak in Colorado, Sears Point in Northern California, and Las Vegas Motor Speedway. Earl and Nicky hit all three, paying an acquaintance to transport the Kawasaki 600. It was a program they knew they couldn't afford over the course of an entire season. "I swear, I felt a lot of pressure," Nicky says. "I knew I needed to do good if I wanted to get a good ride."

In order to get more experience and exposure, Nicky signed up to race the bike in both 600 Supersport and 750 Supersport (another production-based support class, which Tommy rode on his 600). His debut at Pikes was run in the rain, and Nicky finished 12th in 600 and 13th in 750. At Sears, he ran near the front and finished a respectable sixth in a red-flag-affected 600 race, but he didn't do well in the 750 event. He'd had two decent weekends, but he knew he needed something special at the finale in order to land a team ride.

With his shot at a paying ride arguably on the line, Nicky came through. Comfortable on the Vegas track, he qualified well in both classes. It was enough to get him noticed, and although he crashed in the 750 race and finished ninth in the 600 class, Nicky was picked up by Hypercycle Suzuki's Carry Andrew and teamed with Jason Pridmore in 1998. "He had an opportunity to get into a Honda support program for about twice the money, but we had just won the 750 championship," Andrew says. "We were able to give him the attention he deserved, and we got along really well."

Meanwhile, Tommy was having trouble adapting to life on a big-time factory team. After finishing 31st in the '97 Phoenix opener's 600cc race, he sat out Daytona with a dislocated thumb picked up in a practice crash. He posted a strong third-place finish in the Laguna Seca 600 Supersport race, but then he started struggling. An eighth-place finish at Mid-Ohio was a bright spot, but Tommy crashed at Pikes Peak and ground his knee down on the asphalt, forcing him to miss a couple more races. He returned for the final in Vegas but things didn't go well there either.

Tommy picked up the '97 AMA Rookie of the Year award despite his travails, and prior to the '98 season, he drove out to Orange, California, to stay with Muzzy's mechanic Dan Fahie for two months while he tested and trained in the warm weather. "I knew he was going to be coming out, and I figured I'd offer to let him stay at our place," Fahie says. "I used to race, and people have done that for me. I knew that it's so much better when you're staying with someone you know. Plus, we had similar lifestyles, and I just liked him." Fahie would go on to play significant roles in the careers of all three brothers.

It was Christmas break, so Nicky tagged along until he had to go back to school, and the trip became an annual tradition. In 2000, Roger would begin joining his brothers on the winter trips.

"Dan's was like our second home," Tommy remembers. "We had our stuff everywhere, and his wife, Maria, cooked for us every night. In the morning when we woke up, there was a cooler packed for us to take riding for the day. Dan would work on bikes all day for his job, and when he came home, we'd always have something bent up that he'd have to spend an hour on to get us going for the next day. He could hardly get in the garage, with all the stuff we had in there. They bent over backward for us like you wouldn't believe."

The winters in California represented a sort of training camp, with the brothers doing little other than riding motocross at tracks, like Glen Helen Raceway, Lake Elsinore MX Park, Perris Raceway, and Starwest MX, and working out. "We didn't even know how to get anywhere except to the track," Roger says. "There were no distractions, because we didn't have any friends and family, and all we did was get ready for the season."

Riding both the premier class and 600cc Supersport, Tommy posted a couple of podium finishes in '98. Still, he was struggling with learning the tracks and setting his bike up, and he lacked consistency. "I don't really have anyone to blame for that," Tommy says now. "The first little bit—getting to a certain level—came really easy. Then I felt like I just kind of plateaued out, and I had a hard time getting out of that."

Nicky was having an easier time adapting on the Hypercycle team. While Tommy was still winless, Nicky—racing in his first full AMA season—was turning heads with his hard-charging style, occasionally out-braking even the ultra late-braking Miguel Duhamel. Racing in the 600 and 750 classes, he sometimes finished ahead of Yoshimura Suzuki riders Steve Crevier and Aaron Yates, which wasn't always popular with the factory team, but Nicky was under no obligation to play team tactics. By season's end, he had scored five wins in the 750cc Supersport class and one in the 600 division, finishing the year fourth in both classes.

Looking sharp in their TCR team shirts, Rose and Earl watch trackside at the Del Mar Fairgrounds in 1998. Over the years, the parents have followed their children to tracks the world over. (Hayden collection)

"Nicky was just a pleasure to work with," Andrew says. "He always tried so hard, and he would give us great feedback on what the bike was doing. It's easy to say now, but it was true even then—you couldn't ask for a better rider to have on your team."

For the '99 season, Nicky signed a deal with Erion Racing, a satellite squad that served as a farm team for Honda. Although Nicky was racing for Erion, his contract was with Honda, which put him one step closer to the factory team.

Honda racing manager Gary Mathers had first heard about the Haydens several years earlier from American Honda parts manager Brian Uchida, who had sold them parts for their RS125s. Since then, Mathers had met first Earl and then the boys, and he liked what he saw. When a position opened up at Erion, the Haydens were Mathers' first thought. Tommy was taken, so he turned his attention to Nicky, researching his background and contacting his teachers.

"Nicky fit right in because he's got a great family," Mathers says. "They always supported him, and his teachers liked him. I always did look into that stuff, and of course Nicky passed all that with flying colors."

Mathers, who had been responsible for "discovering" Eddie Lawson and Wayne Rainey, also appreciated Nicky's background. "I always thought dirt trackers make good road racers," Mathers says. "One, they're not afraid to go sideways at 100 mph—they've been doing it for years. And the other thing is dirt trackers used to be able to race two, three, four times a week, especially in California and the Midwest."

Mathers theorizes that a 20-year-old dirt tracker will have around 400 races under his belt, whereas a similarly aged road racer might have 40 or 50. When the position opened up, he knew who he wanted, but first he had to convince American Honda vice president Ray Blank, who wanted to hire Kurtis Roberts.

"At Honda, everybody has to agree before anything can happen," Mathers says. "One thing led to another, and I ended up making a pitch to the Japanese. That was over my boss's head, and he didn't like that. Anyway, we were able to hire Nicky, and I was convinced he was going to be good."

Following his brief initial struggle, Nicky seemed to be landing on the right teams, whereas it's possible that Muzzy's hadn't been the ideal place for Tommy to get started. Arguably the strongest squad in the paddock, the team had its focus firmly on Chandler, and there wasn't much time for nurturing an inexperienced rider. Tommy—who was never assigned an official crew chief—was racing in the shadow of the veteran, who had a lot on his plate as he fought for the Superbike title. Tommy had a completely different crew for his second year, and the team didn't invite him to a couple of tests. He was putting a lot of pressure on himself, but because he had nothing to compare his situation to, he wasn't sure what things were supposed to be like.

"I didn't have a *bad* relationship with them," Tommy says of the team. "I guess you could say I just didn't have a relationship at all. They were there and they worked on my bikes, and I thought it was pretty cool. That was about it."

This was especially true of Muzzy himself, a relatively hands-off team owner. Following his original call to Tommy

BELOW: Unsatisfied with just 13 race weekends a year in road racing, Nicky continued to keep his skills sharp racing dirt track. Here he pitches his TCR Harley through a turn at the Del Mar Mile. (Tom Hnatiw)

RIGHT: Nicky at speed at Del Mar in 1998: Gary Nixon served as the assistant manager of the TCR team and helped build Nicky's Harley-Davidson XR750 dirt tracker. (Tom Hnatiw)

In his first sponsored AMA road race effort, Nicky looks resplendent in his new leathers while riding for Carry Andrew's Hypercycle Suzuki during the '98 season. Nicky felt at home immediately on the team and in AMA racing. (Riles/Nelson)

with a job offer, their communication was minimal. Tommy never once visited the race shop, and he only remembers speaking to Muzzy on the phone a couple of times over his first two seasons. Still, Tommy doesn't hold any grudges. "It's not that I would change anything," he says. "It was a big break, and I'm very thankful for that. There were probably better ways to come in if you had your choice, but what are you going to do, turn down the opportunity?"

After all, there were some clear positives to the situation; being thrown in at the deep end taught Tommy to figure things out by himself, which would prove vital in future years. In addition, he got to know Fahie, who was working with Chandler at the time.

Although Tommy had narrowed his focus to road racing upon being hired by Muzzy, Nicky continued to race dirt track. Once he turned 16 in '97, he was eligible to race a 750 twin, which meant he could ride Half-Mile and Mile events in addition to the short track and TT races he was already campaigning on a 500cc Rotax. For the '98 season, Nicky was hired by Tom Cummins Racing (TCR) to campaign a Harley-Davidson XR750 and a Rotax 500 in the GNC races that didn't conflict with his Hypercycle road race duties.

The heroes on that *Motorcycle Man* tape from the Haydens' childhood had all competed simultaneously in both forms of racing, and although the trend among the Haydens' contemporaries had been to specialize in road racing after a certain point in their careers, Nicky was convinced that campaigning the two disciplines helped him to steepen his learning curve. Because he was accustomed to sliding and close-quarters racing in dirt track, he theorized, he wouldn't panic if his road race bike got loose or if he and a competitor inadvertently touched in a corner. And with only about 11 rounds per year in the AMA road race series, racing dirt track kept Nicky sharp.

"It was just racing, competing week in, week out," he says. "I was getting experience going against [Scott] Parker and [Chris] Carr, and as much as anything, I think it helped me get stronger mentally."

Racing in both series also enabled Nicky to set unique goals for himself. For example, he hoped to someday win the Daytona dirt track and the Daytona 200 on the same weekend, and he hoped to become the fifth member of the Grand Slam Club, an unofficial fraternity for the elite few (it included only Dick Mann, Kenny Roberts, Bubba Shobert, and Doug Chandler) who have notched victories in AMA road racing, Short Track, TT, Half-Mile, and Mile competition.

By this time, Nicky's exploits had earned him a nickname. "We always called them the Hayden Wrecking Crew when they came to town, but Nicky needed a name for himself," says Donny Bargmann, who announced the IMDA races with J. B. Norris. "I started calling him the Kentucky Flash, and Earl liked that. I have a photo of the four of us—the three boys and me at Du Quoin—that I still carry in my briefcase. I knew he was going to be going road racing, so I asked him to autograph it, and he signed it 'The Kentucky Flash.' Later I saw that they were calling him the Kentucky Kid in road racing, and I said, 'Gosh darn it, he's no kid; he's the best motorcycle racer in the world. He's a *man* now!'"

Nicky's TCR teammate was Will Davis, a rider he'd been a fan of for years. Nearly blind in one eye (his nickname was Winkin' Will), Davis came from humble beginnings, but he was famous for having heart and a fierce desire to win. Back in June 1989, watching the Lima, Ohio, GNC race the night before an amateur race, Nicky had seen Davis score his first GNC win. Will showed so much emotion on the podium that Nicky began following his career closely, pulling for him to beat Parker. The fact that he rode a Honda for several years—taking on the dominant Harley-Davidsons—was icing on the cake.

With both his brothers now riding for full-on AMA road race teams, Roger was temporarily on his own. Here he wears old leathers and a 2nd Chance Auto logo as he picks up experience in WERA racing. (Riles/Nelson)

Rose bought Nicky one of Davis's official T-shirts (adorned with his personal "Chasin' a Dream" motto), and it had been Nicky's favorite item in his wardrobe for years. He'd gotten to know Will during a couple of Danny Walker's American Supercamps dirt track schools, and now the two were colleagues.

"Will was always a bit of an underdog," Nicky says. "I don't think he was the most talented guy, but he worked so hard to get good. He was always studying everything, and that's something I learned from being around him."

Nicky's first big-bike Grand National was on the Harrington Half-Mile cushion track in Delaware, and during qualifying, Nicky finished ahead of Davis in the semi to qualify for the main. "Will *hated* losing and was pissed," Nicky says, "but instead of being a baby and pouting, he came over and told me two or three places where he was making up time on me, to help me for the main. My respect for him just went up to a whole new level."

For '99, Nicky and Will remained TCR teammates, Nicky again only hitting the rounds that didn't conflict with road race weekends. Nicky finished fifth at the Daytona Short Track season opener, then followed with a runner-up finish at round two's Hagerstown, Maryland, Half-Mile, a result that actually put him on top of the points standings—not only in AMA dirt track, but also in road racing's Supersport class. That GNC lead quickly disappeared when Nicky began missing events to attend road races, but when the GNC series returned to Hagerstown later that season, he posted his first-ever Grand National victory.

The final round was held at Southern California's Del Mar Fairgrounds, a venue whose famously rough, sketchy Mile track played to Nicky's strengths of youth and fitness. Nicky bided his time in the early part of the main event, while Davis and the legendary Parker (in his last-ever race) fought over the lead. Predictably, the track grooved up in turns 1 and 2, while 3 and 4 became rough and slick, and as the race wore on, Nicky's fitness began to come into play. Unfortunately, the race had been shortened from 25 laps to 20, so time was limited.

Nicky inched closer to the two leaders, and with just a few laps remaining, he threw caution to the wind, making up considerable time. Nicky would later call the last three laps some of the best of his life. He passed Davis toward the end (his former teammate would tell him he was nuts for taking such chances on the rough, dangerous track), and set his sights on Parker on the last lap.

"Going into 3, I got sucked in a little bit on the draft, but because of the roost [dirt thrown from the bikes' rear tires], there was no way I was going to draft him to the line," Nicky says. "I had to go for it, but he went in on the very bottom of the groove and left no room."

With Parker protecting the bottom, Nicky tried on the outside; he thought he had it for a moment, but when his back tire came off the groove by a fraction of an inch, Parker came back under. Parker—a popular nine-time champ—had gone out on top, while Nicky had lost out on a chance to add a Mile win to his collection, a blow that was only partly assuaged by his earning the AMA Dirt Track Rookie of the Year award.

"In my opinion, Nicky had so much respect for Scotty and the fact that this was his retirement day," says dirt track announcer J. B. Norris. "I know Scott wouldn't want to hear this, but I think Nicky gave him the opportunity to win his final race."

"I still have nightmares about that," Nicky says. "I don't like ifs and buts, but if I had one race to do over, I'd definitely go up the inside, give him a little love-tap, and push Parker off the groove. They'd probably boo me out of the joint, but it would be worth it."

With a supercross track and empty stands for a backdrop, Tommy's Muzzy racing crew swaps out a front wheel at Daytona in '98. The Haydens had been coming to the city for years to attend amateur dirt track events, but this was the big-time. (Riles/Nelson)

CHAPTER 7

BROTHERS IN ARMS

LEFT: On the Willow Springs Raceway podium with Jamie Hacking (left) and Aaron Yates in 1999, Tommy celebrates his premier AMA road race victory, in the 600cc Supersport class. (Riles/Nelson)
BELOW: While his focus in '99 was on the 600 Supersport title, Nicky also came very close to winning the Formula Xtreme crown as he gained experience with 1000cc machinery. Because No. 69 was unavailable in that class, he opted for No. 169. (Riles/Nelson)

OPPOSITE: Though they appear to agree on hairstyles, the Hayden brothers' minds seem to be in different places during a 1999 test at Laguna Seca. Tommy, Roger, and Nicky's personalities are distinct but congruent. (Tom Hnatiw)

The '99 road racing season brought a fraternal showdown in 600cc Supersport, with Tommy and Nicky going at it all season long. For many outsiders, the tenacity with which the two brothers raced each other was amazing, especially considering how well they appeared to get along off the track, but for No. 22 and No. 69, it wasn't that much different from all those practice sessions on Sunset Downs.

After two years with Muzzy, Tommy had been happy to sign with Yamaha's factory team, which already had a good Superbike presence and—with a brand-new 600 to showcase—was content to have Tommy focus on just the 600 and 750 Supersport classes (both of which he campaigned on the YZF-R6). Tommy was paired with crew chief Tony Romo, with Rich Oliver and Jamie Hacking as his teammates.

"I felt real welcome there, straightaway," Tommy recalls. "I was frustrated, and I was really ready for a change. Tony was my first real crew chief, and I learned stuff from him that I still use today. [Switching teams] gave me a lot of confidence, and I was really excited."

At the same time, Nicky was enthused to be with Erion. He showed up at the season opener at Daytona wearing the treasured No. 69. (Tommy had run No. 169 his first year, but when he became eligible for a two-digit number in '98, No. 69 wasn't available, so he settled for No. 22.) Nicky got off to a better start at Daytona, finishing fourth to winner Miguel Duhamel at round 1, while Tommy was 12th. Nicky then took an impressive win at Phoenix International Raceway's round 2.

The next round was at Southern California's Willow Springs Raceway, a track that Tommy hated, as he hadn't yet gotten comfortable with the treacherous eighth and ninth turns. Tommy stayed with Fahie, who still worked with the Muzzy team, the week before the race, and when they showed up at the track, Tommy was immediately fast. "I'd dreaded going there the whole time because I had struggled in testing," Tommy says, "but somehow it kind of clicked. I really thought I was going to win that day. I knew if I lost, I'd screwed up."

By Saturday, Tommy had quite a bit on everybody, and he qualified

At Pikes Peak in '99, Nicky celebrates winning the Hayden family's first AMA road racing title in 600cc Supersport. Erion Honda had special T-shirts made up with the leopard mascot that Nicky featured on his helmets for some time. (Riles/Nelson)

on pole. On Sunday, he finally scored his debut AMA victory. "That was a huge turning point for me," he says. "It was hard to top that one, especially after how frustrated I'd been. It was the biggest relief ever."

By now, the media had seized upon the unique situation, trying to play the two brothers against each other. Admittedly, it made for a good story, but Tommy and Nicky both insist that they were able to keep the rivalry on the track. "It was the first time the situation really tested things," Tommy recalls. "We were riding as hard as we could and pushing each other, and still—as we had in the past—talking afterward and making it positive. We were making each other better."

The following weekend, it was up to Sonoma for round four at Sears Point, where Tommy had a good race but Nicky scored the win. Laguna Seca was seven days later, and Tommy won in the rain, putting himself back in the points hunt. Nicky won at Road Atlanta, and at Wisconsin's Road America, Jamie Hacking finally broke up the Hayden family party with a win. Nicky and Tommy then traded wins at Loudon and the sea-

son's second Laguna Seca stop. From there, the series headed to Mid-Ohio, a track that had been good to both riders.

"Mid-Ohio used to be patched and rough," Tommy says. "It's tight, and a little untraditional, and I think our background with dirt bikes helps us. Line selection is real important there; you have to be precise."

It was a big weekend for Nicky, who in addition to racing the two Supersport classes on his 600, was also campaigning Formula Xtreme on his 1000 and even substituting for an injured Miguel Duhamel on the factory Honda V4 RC45 Superbike. The Supersport race was a hard battle between Tommy and Nicky, and people still come up to the Haydens and talk about it. "To this day, that was one of the biggest dogfights I've ever been in," Nicky says.

Running together at the front, the brothers traded the lead several times per lap. "That was the first time it was more than just me and him racing each other," Tommy explains. "It was more serious, and there were a lot of other people involved. It wasn't just our own pride at stake; we had companies and teams behind us, and that was different."

One of the questions the Haydens get asked most often is what it feels like to race your brother, and they don't have an easy answer. Although none of them feel that they hold anything back, they do admit it's not the same as racing another adversary. "You always know who it is," Tommy says, "and maybe there's just like a half percent difference in how you do things—so small that you don't even really realize it—but you never really completely forget who it is."

Ultimately, the victory went to Nicky, with Tommy an extremely close second. Hacking picked up another win at Minnesota's Brainerd International Raceway, setting up a last-round face-off between the brothers at Pikes Peak. Unfortunately, Tommy broke his wrist while practicing motocross at home just 10 days before the race, but he had the

BELOW: Having exited the famous Carousel at Sears Point, Nicky and Tommy head toward the top end of the track. The 600cc Supersport class is famous for its close racing. (Tom Hnatiw)

LEFT: Tommy accelerates his Yamaha YZF-R6 out of a turn during a rainy '99 race. Because of his smooth, calculated style, the oldest Hayden brother has always been strong in the wet, a talent he rarely exercises because so few AMA tracks are raced on when it rains. (Riles/Nelson)

BELOW: Tommy leads Nicky during their incredible '99 600cc Supersport battle at Mid-Ohio, a track whose bumpy, technical nature has traditionally been good to the Hayden brothers. "You've got to be precise at that track, and maybe some skill we've picked up over the years makes it easier," Tommy says. (Riles/Nelson)

LEFT: At Laguna Seca Raceway—another strong track for the Hayden brothers—Tommy celebrates another 600 Supersport victory. The AMA visited the track twice in 1999, and Tommy won on both occasions. (Riles/Nelson)

Following a race, a slightly leery Tommy makes an appearance with a contingent of enthusiastic Hayden supporters, some of whom are family friends from Owensboro. The brothers have always enjoyed strong fan support. (Riles/Nelson)

wrist pinned and competed anyway. Tommy even managed a second-place finish, but the win went to Aaron Yates, while Nicky finished fifth to beat Tommy for the title by just eight points. Nicky also made the podium in the Superbike race.

"That was my first title, so it will always be kind of special," Nicky says. "The 600 class is so important to the manufacturers that it feels good to win, and we went at it the whole distance, which is always good."

That same season, Nicky had also done well in Formula Xtreme (a support class that then fielded hopped-up 1000s). He won seven out of 10 races (and every round in which his bike didn't break), finishing second in the year-end points. In addition to his AMA Flat Track Rookie of the Year honor that season, Nicky was also named AMA Athlete of the Year, an award open to racers in all disciplines. It had definitely been a breakthrough year for the 18-year-old.

Honda knew a good thing when they saw it, and they quickly promoted Nicky from Erion to the factory team for the 2000 season. "It was an easy decision," says Gary Mathers. "He's a real likable guy, real easy to work with. We'd let him down once in a while, but he'd say, 'Well, I screwed up last week, so it's your turn.' He was just nice—real personable—and he always tried hard. And he hates to lose—I mean, *hates* it, which is important."

As is often the case with younger siblings, Roger always sought the approval of his older brothers, and their accomplishments became his goals. And as is often the case between oldest and youngest siblings, Tommy and Roger didn't always see eye to eye. They loved each other and wanted the best for each other, but communicating could sometimes be difficult.

"If Rog has a problem," Dan Fahie explains, "he doesn't want to go to Tommy—even if he knows he can figure it out—because Tommy will probably beat him up about it a little bit.

He'll go to Nick, and Nick will say, 'Ah, I don't know.' So then they both go to Tommy and ask, 'How do we fix this?' and nine times out of ten, Tommy will fix it."

After Nicky had turned pro in '98, Roger had been left on his own for a year in the Amateur ranks, where he tried his best to live up to the lofty exploits of his older brothers. His last name was both a blessing and a curse, and sometimes, it was difficult for Roger to earn respect. Slightly overweight at the time, he had picked up the unflattering nickname Porkchop, which was rather unfair considering the success Roger was enjoying in his own right. In Indy, at that year's AMA Amateur Nationals (later renamed the Dirt Track Grand Championships), Roger survived a hard crash to keep the Dirt Track Horizon Award in the family. "It was a little bit of a bigger deal the second year," Roger remembers, "and I wanted it because Nicky had got it. It was pretty cool to have two brothers get the same award."

With the parents sometimes occupied tending to Tommy and Nicky's careers, the youngest Hayden brother would occasionally hitch rides to the races with other racers—Nick Daniels for dirt track and Robert Zerbisias for road races—although it wasn't unusual for Earl to drive all night from a pro race to see Rog take part in a club event.

Roger would begin riding for a dirt track team called Maroney's at the end of '99, but the goal was to get him into road racing—something the Haydens' finite funds had thus far not allowed him to do to any great extent. With his 16th birthday approaching in May 1999, the family began talking him up. By now, the Haydens had built up a strong network of contacts among the racing teams, and promoting Roger was their mutual project. "At one point, Rog hadn't even ridden a 600 yet, but we were going, 'Yeah, he's *good* on a four-stroke!'" Nicky says with a laugh.

The family's persistence—and Nicky's past experience

with Suzuki—opened doors for Roger, who began getting backdoor help through Hypercycle. When he turned 16, Roger signed a deal to complete the season with a Suzuki satellite team run by a Northern California shop called Cycle Gear. One week later, he raced his first AMA event during round 5 at Road Atlanta. Running No. 169, Roger finished fifth in 750cc Supersport—the best AMA debut of any of the Hayden brothers. For the rest of that season, he alternated between road races and dirt track rounds in the GNC series, struggling with crashes on both circuits.

The success of Roger's brothers had been helpful in landing him sponsorship, but it also brought the pressure of certain expectations. "It was tough," he says. "I was pretty inexperienced, and that year, I probably crashed two or three times a weekend. It definitely played with my mind a little bit, but Cycle Gear never gave up on me. I still have a lot of respect for them."

Roger stayed with Maroney's for dirt track in 2000, but for his road racing efforts, he switched to Chaparral Suzuki, a satellite team run out of a Southern California dealership. The team was led by respected tuner Kel Carruthers, who had wrenched Kenny Roberts and Eddie Lawson to a combined six world titles. Roger led a couple of 750cc Supersport races and made his first podium finish at Laguna Seca, in front of a big audience during the World Superbike/AMA Superbike weekend.

"That was real big," Roger recalls. "It gave me some confidence, and I was a lot better everywhere we went after that."

Racing was unquestionably the focus in the Haydens' lives, but the brothers also knew how to have fun away from the track. In fact, such recesses were necessary in order to remain fresh and focused when they turned up at the races. "You can only think about racing, riding, and training so much," Nicky explains. "Sometimes you've got to just force yourself to go do something different."

One weekend every year, Nicky and Roger would drive up to Keeneland to watch the horse races or to Lexington to visit sister Jenny or their friend Clint Simmons. Both were enrolled at the University of Kentucky, and hanging out there exposed the Hayden boys to a way of life that although normal for most kids, was completely foreign to them. They would socialize, eat lunch in the school cafeteria, and attend basketball and football games. They enjoyed themselves, but they were not tempted to send in their applications.

"It was fun to see another side of life, with the fraternities and all," Nicky says, "but by Sunday, I could pretty well tell that it wasn't for me. It reminded me how good it was to be doing what we were doing."

Although college wasn't in the plans for the Hayden brothers, Earl and Rose were adamant that they must finish high school. Classes had gone fairly easily for Tommy, who had graduated from Owensboro Catholic High in '96 before signing with his first big team. The younger Hayden brothers, however, were already successful racers while in high school, and perhaps not coincidentally, they were more likely to get into trouble—often together.

In fact, if Roger's surname had opened doors in the racing world, it was decidedly less beneficial in the classroom: "The first day of high school, when they called our names, all the teachers asked if I was Nicky's brother," Roger remembers. "I'd say yes, and they'd put me in the desk right in front of theirs. By the end of the first day, I was saying, 'No, I'm not his brother.'"

Typically pragmatic, Tommy had behaved not because he was an angel but simply to avoid punishment. "I didn't like the hassle of getting in trouble," he admits. "I didn't like being in school in the first place; the last thing I wanted to do was stay

BELOW: Earl consults with his son on Laguna Seca's pit wall in 1999, one year after Nicky took his first AMA road racing win at the venue. (Tom Hnatiw)

LEFT: A rolling burnout signals another 600 Supersport success for Nicky. Although the Haydens are careful to avoid boastfulness, their absolute love of winning can make for spectacular victory celebrations. (Riles/Nelson)

Sporting spots worthy of his leopard mascot, Nicky flashes his trademark smile in the Laguna paddock. (Tom Hnatiw)

another hour for detention. It was just a big inconvenience, and I always felt like I had stuff to do."

The situation was different for Nicky and Roger. Although their classmates may not have had a full appreciation for their stardom, the brothers were taking red-eye flights back from races and missing school tests to attend bike tests. Not surprisingly, they sometimes had trouble paying attention in class, and—following the examples of their fun-loving mechanics–they occasionally pulled pranks that resulted in Earl having to visit his boys in the principal's office.

Not that they always got caught: Once, Nicky and Roger stuck a red police light on their car and pulled the basketball squad's team bus over as it was returning from an away basketball game. The Haydens were good-looking boys, a fact that didn't escape the notice of Jenny's friends or the girls at the racetracks. It wasn't uncommon for the brothers and their friends to "borrow" Dad's keys and entertain their dates at 2nd Chance Auto, but steady girlfriends were a rarity. On a couple occasions, Gary Nixon tried to set Tommy up with his daughter but to no avail.

When the boys were younger, Earl had seen a racer named Lance Jones (a young dirt tracker he had helped for a while) go down the wrong path, and he regularly warned his boys about the adverse effects that alcohol, drugs, and girls could have on their racing careers. Even swearing was strictly forbidden.

The Hayden sisters came in handy for more than just helping their brothers meet girls. Both were good students, and Roger remembers having Kathleen type his papers in exchange for rides to school, when he was a senior and she was a freshman. "I'd get better grades than my friends!" he says with a laugh.

By the time he was a junior, Nicky was winning AMA Supersport races, signing six-figure contracts, and driving a new truck, so if he was occasionally distracted in class, it was no wonder. "I'd be getting ready to fly off to Daytona," he says, "and I just couldn't make time to go to the library for a couple of hours to do research and an outline for a six-page paper. It was hard for me to just sit there when my mind was focused on racing."

With tutors helping to keep them on track, Nicky and Roger graduated in 2000 and 2001, respectively. Looking back, Nicky says that when he travels around the world, he regrets not knowing a foreign language, and Tommy wishes he didn't have to spell-check every letter he writes.

That said, all three Hayden boys are happy they stuck it out. They have good memories from those days, and they still hang out with their old school buddies. "I'm glad we went to a real school, and not homeschooling," Tommy says. "That was real good for us, and it gave us as normal a childhood as we could expect. I think it's good that we didn't miss out on that."

STUMBLING BLOCKS

Things were moving quickly for all of the Hayden brothers. All three were racing at the pro level (two on factory teams) and appeared destined for greatness. But it would have to be earned, and a reminder of that came at the 2000 Daytona season opener. Nicky's bike suffered a cracked header pipe near the end of the feature and lost by just a hundredth of a second, with Mat Mladin taking advantage of the draft to the finish line to score his first Daytona 200 victory. Tommy finished seventh in the same race.

It was a heartbreaking loss for Nicky, now 18, but in nearly winning the first race in his first full AMA Superbike season, the young racer had made a point: "Nicky Hayden's second-place finish not only gained him respect in the sport," Don Emde wrote in *Daytona 200: The History of America's Premier Motorcycle Race*, "but also marked him as a serious new competitor. Since 1991, with the exception of the 1993 race . . . Scott Russell and Miguel Duhamel had dominated the Daytona 200. A new era had indeed begun."

Mladin won the next two races as well, gaining an early advantage in the points, but Nicky got a shot in the arm at Wisconsin's Road America. It was mechanic Davey Jones who first noticed that there was something special about Nicky's riding during practice and qualifying that June weekend. Nicky was on the grid for the first race in a doubleheader when Jones patted him on the back and looked into his eyes: "Hey, today is your day," Jones said, and with that, the bikes were started and the mechanics walked off the grid.

Up-and-coming racers dream of landing a factory ride with any major squad, but Honda is considered the Holy Grail. No other team can match the financial and technical resources that Big Red has at its disposal, and the manufacturer has a deserved reputation for realizing virtually any objective its management and engineers set their minds on.

What their minds were on at the moment was a championship in AMA Superbike, the top road racing class in the country. Since the division's 1976 inception, Honda had taken the championship seven

different times, with great names like Fred Merkel, Wayne Rainey, Bubba Shobert, and Miguel Duhamel (Nicky's teammate). Ben Bostrom had won it for them in 1998, and with Yoshimura Suzuki's Mladin having wrested it away, Honda was counting on Nicky or Duhamel to take it back.

This was Nicky's first full year in the class, although he had gotten experience the previous season by substituting for the injured Duhamel at four races (including the finale at Pikes Peak, where he'd made the podium). He was riding Honda's new V-twin RC51, and there was a lot to learn; factory superbike riders have a wider range of tires from which to choose, and their bikes feature electronics that acquire reams of data for interpretation by the crew.

Upon Nicky's promotion from Erion in 2000, Honda had put him under the tutelage of famed crew chief Merlyn Plumlee, with family friend Dan Fahie (who, a couple years earlier, had moved from Muzzy Kawasaki to Honda to work with Eric Bostrom) working as a chassis mechanic on the 600 and Jones serving as chassis technician on the superbike. It was a championship-caliber crew. "The nice thing about working with Nick is he's a real, straightforward, pure racer," Plumlee says. "There aren't a lot of head games, and he doesn't have to have a psychologist for a crew chief. That's never been my strong point; I've always been better with riders who are here to do a job and know how to do the job, and they don't need a lot of coddling. Nick's very much that way, and we communicated well too. We got along immediately, and the team would do anything for him."

The crew's first step was to get Nicky a win, and that Road America race was a prime opportunity. Most of it was a back-and-forth affair between a small group of riders, but toward the end, Nicky took over the lead. That's when his mechanic's parting words came back into his mind. "I remember getting really excited," Nicky says, "because I knew Davey was right

and that I really did have a chance to get my first win. I just thought, 'Hey, I've got to put in the cleanest laps of my life right here.'"

Nicky stayed strong to the end, scoring the win, and then proving it wasn't a fluke by notching another victory the following day. No matter what happened now, everyone knew that Nicky was for real.

Nicky followed another defeat to Mladin in New Hampshire with a win at Laguna Seca. Next came victories by Duhamel and Aaron Yates, but Nicky was still in contention for the title. He and Duhamel had been sharing a spare superbike, but now Honda dedicated two machines to Nicky and had him stop campaigning Supersport.

Things looked good, but after building a huge lead at Pikes Peak's next-to-last round, Nicky was struck by a fluke tire problem, and his subsequent fifth-place result ended realistic hope of attaining the title. He finished the year with a win at the Willow Springs finale, and while Mladin took his second AMA Superbike title, Nicky ended up just five points back in second. Nicky was extremely frustrated to miss out on the crown, and he was disappointed to go winless in Supersport. Nonetheless, it had been a very solid rookie season.

"Everything went really smooth that year," Nicky says. "Luckily I had Merlyn Plumlee for a crew chief, and he really made things easy on me. He's really sharp and has a lot of knowledge, and he helped me learn the bike, the tires, and the class. I think we did better than the team expected, and even better than I expected."

Within the team, the topic of Nicky's future began to turn up in discussions. It was no secret that the international stage was his target, and American Honda wanted to help him get there.

Still riding for Yamaha, Tommy finished the year sixth

BELOW: Nicky slides his XR750 at Del Mar in 2001. He and Roger both rode for a Dave Burks-managed team with sponsorship from Samson Exhaust Systems and Corbin Motors, but neither would win an AMA GNC round that year. (Tom Hnatiw)

RIGHT: Look closely and you can see Nicky working a thumb-operated rear brake in this photo. His dirt track experience made him fond of the rear brake, and this system made using the rear brake easier in right-hand corners, where his boot might otherwise touch the ground. When Nicky eventually got to MotoGP, the Japanese convinced him not to use the thumb brake. (Riles/Nelson)

in Superbike points, fourth in 600cc Supersport. Riding for Chaparral Suzuki, Roger Lee ended the season fifth in 750cc Supersport, earning a 2001 ride with Bruce Transportation Group, a small Honda satellite team.

Meanwhile, Nicky continued to hit Grand National dirt track events when race dates didn't conflict with his road racing. Few people are aware that Nicky was actually offered a dirt track contract with Harley-Davidson, an arrangement that would have seen him simultaneously riding for two different factory teams. The process went as far as Gary Howard negotiating a salary, but Honda understandably nixed the arrangement and Nicky continued with Tom Cummings Racing.

"Tom Cummings really believed in me and gave me the opportunity to be a part-time dirt tracker," Nicky says. "I had to miss a lot of races because of my road racing, but he always made sure I had a good bike." The fact that Honda accepted Nicky's part-time dirt track racing was unusual in the modern era, because most factories feared the rider's increased risk of injury in a series outside his primary focus. With the influential Gary Mathers in favor of the arrangement, however, Nicky was safe. Both Nicky and his manager felt that dirt track kept him sharp for road racing, and his results were strong in both series. That season, Nicky made the top 10 in year-end dirt track points, but more important, he won the Springfield Short Track. That feat—when combined with his previous season's Half-Mile win and his road race victories—put him over halfway to the prestigious Grand Slam. All he needed now were wins in TT and Mile events.

With the success came more changes. Nicky signed a deal to wear road racing leathers made by Joe Rocket, a then-relatively unknown company from Canada, eager to establish a presence in America. To make the most of their new in-vestment, Rocket shot a television commercial based around Nicky in May.

That same year, Nicky celebrated his high school graduation by moving out of his parents' house—kind of. Unprepared for the hassles of living completely on his own, Nicky instead transferred into a small-but-comfortable space above the family's new garage, giving him some independence but leaving him just across the driveway from Rose's meals.

In addition to the garage, Earl and Rose—whose finances had finally been given a break by Tommy and Nicky's factory contracts—had built a swimming pool, added onto the house, and expanded their property. With International Racers' help, the family was also investing in rental property around Owensboro (they currently own nearly 100 units), and Nicky and Tommy purchased a 90-acre plot of land adjoining their parents' home. In 2000, Tommy bought his own house and moved out.

"I was ready to have something of my own," Tommy says. "It was something I'd had on my mind for a while. There were a lot of things I liked about living at home, but my room looked like a storage closet, with boxes and stuff stacked everywhere. I just needed some more space, and it was a pretty good investment too." That said, Tommy's place is just a few miles away, and between meals and riding, he visits his parents almost every day.

Meanwhile, Roger continued living in the boys' childhood bedroom, still covered in racing posters.

The first year of the new millennium had gone well for the Haydens, with the notable exception of the return flight from the final AMA Superbike race. Tommy had made other travel plans, but Earl and Rose were accompanied by Nicky, Roger, Kathleen, family friends Clint Simmons and Seth Lawson (Nicky's lab partner in high school and now an employee

at 2nd Chance Auto), and cousin Eddie Thompson—a former racer and one of the brothers' biggest fans, who had also helped them occasionally throughout their careers.

After landing in Memphis, the group transferred to a Northwest Airlines flight that was to terminate in Owensboro after a stopover in Paducah, Kentucky. Flush with their success at California's Willow Springs, the group was laughing and joking on the small plane, and when the flight attendant took exception to the ruckus, it only added fuel to the fire for a couple of the people. "She thought everybody was drunk," Roger explains, "but we were just kind of having fun. Our mom was with us, and most of the people hadn't had anything to drink."

When the small plane had a rough landing in Paducah, Roger drew laughs by digging his helmet out of the overhead storage compartment and buckling it on. Irritated, the flight attendant didn't allow Kathleen to use the bathroom during the layover, and when the plane was back in the air, she turned up the heat and refused to serve sodas or water to the group. This of course prompted more horseplay from the kids, but Rose's presence ensured that the jokes didn't get too far out of line. "We weren't completely innocent," Nicky admits. "We gave her a bit of a hard time, but we weren't drinking."

Nonetheless, the police were waiting when the plane landed in Owensboro, the pilot having radioed ahead at the insistence of the flight attendant, who told the officers that she had been assaulted and that minors had been drinking. As is mandatory in such cases, a federal investigation was opened, and the Haydens were banned from the airline.

An article on the incident appeared in the local paper the next day, and Seth—an honor student who had told his teachers his absence had been caused by sickness—got into some trouble when it became clear he'd actually been at a motorcycle race. Concerned Honda officials also got word of the story and called the Haydens to check it out.

The Haydens knew they were innocent of any serious wrongdoing, but they were also aware that their professional reputations could be damaged even *without* a guilty verdict. International Racers got involved, and the case was quickly settled out of court, without the Haydens being charged. Aiding their case was the fact that the flight attendant had called the police on other occasions, but the biggest assistance was the testimony of two respectable elderly ladies—one of whom was involved in city politics—who had also been passengers on the flight. Northwest wrote the Haydens a letter of apology, paid their legal fees, and removed their ban from the airline.

Nicky's sophomore Superbike year got off to a rough start, as he broke his navicular or scaphoid bone during pre-season testing. In the 2001 Daytona Supersport race, Roger crashed and left oil on the track, and with officials being late to display a red flag, Nicky—racing with a still-broken wrist—hit the slick spot and crashed as well, though he still managed a runner-up finish after the restart. In the Daytona 200, Nicky was riding well until a bearing failed in his motor. He pushed his dead RC51 to pit lane, however, and a red flag allowed him to reenter on a second bike. The race was marred by more red flags and a dangerous pace-car incident, but Nicky eventually managed a 10th-place finish, with Mladin scoring his second 200 win in a row.

That put Nicky, who underwent wrist surgery the very next day, at an immediate points deficit, which grew as the year progressed. Nicky's mechanic Davey had injured his back and was out for the whole season, so Mark Braunwalder was brought in to fill his place. Nicky came out second to Anthony Gobert in an incredible battle at Sears Point, but at Road

Atlanta, electrical problems struck during qualifying, and Nicky crashed in the race while trying to make up for his poor grid position. Rear-brake troubles struck at Road America, and, to make matters worse, Nicky had begun experiencing problems with carpal tunnel syndrome, a common malady among motorcycle racers. Nicky was winless through the entire first half of the season, and the second half started with a crash at the newly renamed Mazda Raceway Laguna Seca. Something was obviously wrong.

"That was really a low point in my career," Nicky sighs. "I remember when I was going back to my hotel that night, I thought I was done. I was wondering if I would ever win another race. It was pretty depressing."

The losses were getting Nicky down, but his tight-knit crew rallied around him. Eager to restore his rider's confidence, Fahie decided something needed to be done. Next on the schedule was the Mid-Ohio doubleheader, and the week before the race, he invited Nicky to fly out to visit him in California. Together, they loaded a 600 into a van and drove up to Buttonwillow Raceway Park, near Bakersfield, for a local track day.

"It was a tough time in my career," Nicky remembers. "When you put a lot into things but it still feels like the wheels are coming off, it sucks, so I just spent the week going back to the basics and riding the bike, trying to have some fun: no fancy semis, catered lunches, or anything else—just me and Dan-o, out in the desert putting down laps."

The fresh approach on the smaller bike was just what Nicky needed, and he won the second race in Ohio. Next came victories at the last three races of the season, at Minnesota's Brainerd International Raceway, Colorado's Pikes Peak International Raceway, and Virginia International Raceway (VIR). He also earned the pole position at Pikes Peak by posting the fastest lap during qualifying; surprisingly, it was the

first pole of his Superbike career, and it represented a big step for Nicky.

"I wasn't a great qualifier in my early AMA days," Nicky admits. "That whole one-lap thing took a while to learn, and Mat [Mladin] was king at that. I definitely had to work on that quite a lot."

Nicky finished third in the year, 30 points behind Mladin, with Eric Bostrom second. Once again, he was frustrated to have lost out on the title to Mladin, who had told him that the path to the Grand Prix World Championship series led through him, but Nicky had a lot of respect for his rival. "I definitely believe [Mat] made me a better racer," Nicky says.

Nicky's dirt track season didn't go any better. Riding with Roger for a team that was sponsored by Samson and Corbin, he again hit GNC events that didn't conflict with the road races, and he went winless in the year. Although Nicky made a point not to let the hectic schedule handicap his road racing, it couldn't have helped his dirt track performances. Following one Honda test at Willow Springs, he grabbed a red-eye flight to Springfield, hailed a taxi to the hotel for a shower, and showed up at the fairgrounds without having slept. That night, he got a bad start in the main, charged to the front, and barely got beat to the line by Bryan Bigelow. "I *still* feel bitter about that!" Nicky says. "He had been an amateur rival of mine, and that was his first win. It was a nail-biter, and I hated losing it."

At the Lima Half-Mile, Nicky failed to even make the main, but the semi-race battle with Jess Roeder was one for the ages, with the two trading positions multiple times per lap. At the end, Nicky was a close second, not good enough to qualify. Roeder, who calls it one of the most special races of his career, says strangers still tell him it was the best race they've ever seen.

Another close race happened at the Springfield TT, where

Nicky faced his older brother in the main. Tommy hadn't competed in a single dirt track event since 1996, but Nicky talked him into bringing his self-prepared Yamaha YZ426F out to Springfield to try and revitalize an unsatisfying season. "I wasn't really sure how a DTX bike would work," Tommy says, "but I decided to do it. I went there, and it turned out the track was basically built for my bike."

Uncooperative weather had forced organizers to reschedule the race to Monday, but Tommy didn't mind. Despite a displacement handicap to the 500s (including Nicky's Rotax), his bike was actually an advantage in the tight turns and over the jumps, and he and his brother had an incredible battle. In the end, Tommy took his first Grand National victory despite runner-up Nicky's best efforts. "I grew up dirt-tracking, and it's always been my first love," Tommy says. "I always wanted to win some nationals doing that, and to finally be able to do that, it was definitely one of the more memorable races that I've ever had."

"Some of the guys were sitting there with their framers, thinking, 'What do we do now?' " announcer Donny Bargmann says. "Tommy showed that a DTX bike could be pretty competitive—maybe even an advantage."

For Nicky, the low point of the season came a few months later, when he lost his friend and former teammate, Will Davis—killed on Saturday night, August 25, 2001, at the Sedalia, Missouri, Grand National Championship race. Davis crashed in turn 4 of the first lap in the main event, and several other racers went down as well. Doctors at Bothwell Regional Hospital cited multiple traumas as the cause of death for Davis, who left behind a wife and son.

When Nicky (who had borrowed Davis's extra bike at the Peoria TT the week before) heard the news, he was in a hotel room in Colorado, where he was attending the Pikes Peak AMA Superbike national. "The next morning was the first time

I ever woke up and didn't really care about going to the track," he says. "It hits you pretty hard when your friend, mentor, and former teammate gets killed the night before a big race."

When Nicky showed up at the team semi, Plumlee sat him down and had a talk. "There's no shame in getting killed doing what you love to do," the crew chief said.

Nicky, who calls Davis "as hungry to win as any guy I'd ever been around," was inspired, and after winning the Pikes Peak race, he rode a lap backward in honor of Davis. He also adopted Davis's "Chasin' a Dream" motto as his own.

It was a tough year, and not just for Nicky, as Tommy and Roger also struggled in 2001. After Tommy and Nicky had battled so hard in '99, the oldest Hayden brother had hit a drought through the following two seasons, with his Springfield TT win being the one bright spot. At season's end, Yamaha told Tommy they'd be replacing him for the following year.

When asked if losing the 600cc Supersport title to his younger brother could possibly have affected his confidence, Tommy thinks for several seconds. "I can't say it didn't," he admits. "I didn't notice that, but maybe subconsciously it took something away. It definitely seemed like I was missing something those two years."

Meanwhile, Roger, who graduated from high school that season, was still learning the ropes of professional road racing. Now running No. 95, he had ridden two classes that season: Supersport and Formula Xtreme. Although he immediately felt comfortable on the big bikes (perhaps because of his dirt track background) and even made the occasional podium, he was having problems. Like Nicky, Roger was suffering from carpal tunnel syndrome, and after the Formula USA Del Mar dirt track (the last race of the year), the two flew up to San Francisco with Rose to have Dr. Arthur Ting perform corrective surgery on their wrists.

CHAPTER 9 | TITLE TIME

Despite an unsatisfactory 2001, Nicky's wins at the last four AMA Superbike races meant that he had the momentum going into the off-season. After a quick recovery from his surgery for carpal tunnel syndrome, he was going fast in testing, and Mat Mladin soon began complaining to the press that Nicky's 1000cc twin had an unfair advantage over his 750cc four. Mladin is renowned for getting into his rivals' heads, but Nicky didn't mind one bit. "Actually, that's when I started to get an edge on him," he reveals. "Honestly, seeing those comments helped my head. It just made me think that I had him beat before the season even started."

Nicky's first chance to try out his renewed confidence would come at the March 10, 2002, Daytona 200. The race has been held annually since 1937, missing just four years in the '40s for World War II. The original, 3.7-mile course was literally on Daytona Beach, with riders racing north up the sand and then south down Highway A1A, but in 1961 it was moved into the then-new Daytona International Speedway. The exact circuit has changed several times, but for the most part, it has combined part of the facility's famous (and treacherous) banking and an infield section.

Informally known as America's motorcycle race, the Daytona 200 has attracted top racers from America and abroad, and although it has lost some of its prestige in the modern era, a win in that race was still worth at least three times more to a rider in terms of bonuses (easily in the six-figure region) than any other AMA Superbike event, not to mention the cachet.

The Daytona 200 is a unique event in the AMA Superbike series in that as the only endurance round, its 200-mile distance is three times longer than the typical national. As a result, Superbike teams must organize pit stops, where bikes are refueled and fitted with fresh tires. (The support classes run shorter races, under the typical sprint-race format.)

Nicky came into the 2002 race hungry and ready, fresh off a productive winter at Dan Fahie's unofficial boot camp. During qualifying, he

took a spill that he still suspects was caused by a bad tire. The fall was immortalized in video shot for television coverage from a bike-mounted camera. "That was one of the biggest high sides I've ever had in my life!" Nicky says.

Nicky banged his head and foot in the incident, and the medication that doctors gave him for the swelling kept him awake all Thursday night. He was still dizzy the next morning, so he opted not to practice for the Supersport class (the 600cc class dropped the displacement from its official name that year, and the 750cc Supersport class was renamed as Superstock). Despite the problems, Nicky still managed to qualify on pole in both Superbike (earning a $10,000 Rolex watch) and Supersport, and since Mladin had also crashed hard in practice and suffered an elbow injury that put him out of the 200, Nicky's chances for success looked particularly good.

In the weekend's feature, Nicky diced with Anthony Gobert, Kurtis Roberts, and Miguel Duhamel early on, then put his head down and pulled away. He got some help in the form of motor problems for his teammate Duhamel, and

Roberts destroyed his tire. Nicky's winning margin over runner-up Jamie Hacking was 18.255 seconds.

"Daytona was real special," Nicky says. "It's a race I grew up dreaming about and watching my heroes race. I even once got caught sneaking in underage with the wrong pass that my brother passed through the fence to me! I knew I wanted to go to Grand Prix, but a 200 win is one of those things I needed on the wall, along with a Superbike title. Daytona's where it all started, and that place has lots of history and is just special. And after getting so close my rookie year, I didn't want any unfinished business on this side. Also, I was really happy for my team."

On the cool-down lap, Nicky noticed a group of dirt trackers waving at him from the infield, where they were watching from on top of the motor home of racer Paul Lynch. "I guess they weren't too impressed, though," Nicky says with a laugh. "A bunch of them had their pants down around the ankles, mooning me! I wouldn't expect anything less from my dirt trackers!"

It was a great start to the season, and Nicky was feeling more at home than ever—in the Superbike class, and with Honda. "What I liked best about that year was my team," Nicky says, speaking of Merlyn Plumlee and Dan Fahie (who by now were almost like a father and brother to Nicky), Davey Jones (who had recovered from his back injury), Daisuke Hashimoto (who handled the suspension), and Darrin Marshall (who had been brought in to handle data acquisition for both Nicky and Duhamel). "I had that group of people around me, and that makes a big difference," Nicky continues. "Having good guys isn't enough; you've got to have the *right* guys. They believed in me, and I wanted to win for them. It made it fun."

"It was a really nice chemistry," Plumlee concurs. "All the guys had a great time, and it was certainly the highlight of my career."

The late-afternoon sun highlights Roger's Erion Honda CBR as he negotiates a turn. (Riles/Nelson)

That said, there were already thoughts of breaking up the harmonious crew. Less than an hour after Nicky's Daytona 200 victory, International Racers' Steven Dicterow spoke with his rider. "Gee, Nicky, I'm really sorry," was his first, tongue-in-cheek comment. "That could be the last time you ever race Daytona."

Dicterow was referring to the fact that the performance had put Nicky on the radar of teams competing on the World Championship Grand Prix circuit, Nicky's desired destination since he had started riding.

"We were looking at GPs and World Superbike," says American Honda racing manager Chuck Miller, who replaced Gary Mathers. "There was talk about what his next step would be, and whether he could be the next Bubba [Shobert] or Wayne [Rainey] or Randy [Mamola]—any of the stars that have come here and then gone on to world racing."

Of course, getting on the radar was one thing, but landing a premier-class ride would require backing up the Daytona victory. At any rate, Nicky didn't want to move on from the American championship before taking a Superbike title, something he felt was important for his confidence.

As it turned out, Daytona was the 2002 season in a nutshell, as everything clicked for Nicky. He lost the next race at California Speedway, but the event was a weekend doubleheader and Nicky came out on top on day two. Next came a dominant doubleheader weekend at Sears Point (which had just changed its name to Infineon Raceway) followed by another one at Road Atlanta. With seven races in the books, Nicky had won six.

At that point, the prudent thing to do was to ride smart and protect the considerable championship lead, as the AMA points system rewards consistency and punishes DNFs (did not finish). "Really, the second half of the season wasn't as exciting," Dicterow says. "With the championship to consider,

Nicky couldn't take as many chances anymore; he just had to make sure he finished high enough in the points."

Nonetheless, Nicky would still have opportunities for more fun that year.

After leaving Yamaha the previous season, Tommy had received several offers for 2002, including a couple of options to race in World Supersport (a 600-based international support class to World Superbike). The most attractive deal, however, was from Kawasaki. As with his initial Yamaha contract, this one would have Tommy focusing on just one bike—the ZX-6R—in Supersport and Superstock, something that was appealing to Tommy. Adding to the temptation was the fact that Eric Bostrom had just ridden the bike to the 2001 Supersport championship.

Tommy had considered riding for Kawasaki in 2000, after his first year with Yamaha. Kawasaki team manager Mike Preston had given him a good offer that would have teamed him with Doug Chandler again, and although Tommy decided to stick with Yamaha at that time, he and Preston had enjoyed a good relationship and stayed in touch ever since.

Tommy decided to take the Kawasaki deal, and he and Roger also both signed contracts with Joe Rocket leathers, joining Nicky with the growing brand. In May, a crew traveled to California to shoot another commercial at Fahie's house. (When the mechanic got home from work that day, he found his furniture was all out on the front lawn!)

Excited to get a fresh start, Tommy was that much more motivated, and his winter testing went well. Heading up Tommy's crew was Joey Lombardo, who had previously served as chassis mechanic on Bostrom's Superbike. This was Lombardo's first time in the role of crew chief, but because he and Tommy had known each other for years, the adjustment period was relatively easy. Lombardo had worked

Nicky at his "side job" again in 2002, pitching his Honda into a Springfield Short Track corner on his way to the win. Of the six Grand National victories in Nicky's career, four came at Springfield. (Flat Trak Fotos)

with Honda in the past, so he also got some advice from his friend Fahie.

"Joey and I talked quite a bit," Fahie says. "I remember standing on the motor home that year at the Springfield Mile, talking about Tommy—what his likes and dislikes are, how best to handle stuff, and how to communicate with him."

From Joey's perspective, he was fortunate to be assigned the analytical Tommy—still a decent mechanic in his own right—as his first rider. "He's patient, he's easy to talk to, and he's good at communicating what he wants," Joey says. "He's serious, and he's always got a plan in his head. He doesn't require much in the way of mental coaching or pep talks."

It turned out to be a good fit, and 2002 was a sort of rebound year for Tommy. It started off rough with a big crash at Daytona, but the next round saw him break his drought at California Speedway with a Superstock win.

That win, combined with Nicky's Superbike victory at the same venue, had people talking about the possibility of all

three Hayden brothers scoring podium finishes on the same weekend in their various road race classes—or better yet, winning. For that to happen, though, things would have to start going better for Roger.

Part of the reason for Roger's struggle was mechanical problems outside his control, but the finger was often pointed at him. "They were saying I was back-shifting too quick and stuff like that," Roger says, "but I haven't ever changed the way I ride a bike, and I haven't had those problems on other teams."

Roger scored a runner-up finish in Formula Xtreme at Road Atlanta, and taking Nicky's Superbike double there into account, as well as Tommy's third-place finish in the 600cc class, it was a sort of Hayden podium triple, though not the kind they were shooting for.

Roger had hoped that getting into the Honda farm system would pay dividends, as it had with Nicky, but the situation was actually hurting him. Although he got along well with team manager Rick Hobbs, he clashed with owner Kevin Erion, which was anything but politically beneficial.

"Things went okay for the first little bit," Roger says, "but I tore the meniscus in my knee playing basketball and missed Sears Point. I had a mechanic I really liked, and he got fired while I was hurt. After that, it pretty much just went downhill. I had lots of mechanicals, and it was all blamed on me."

While Tommy rode Supersport and Superstock and Roger rode Supersport and Formula Xtreme, Nicky—at Honda's request—had streamlined his post-Daytona efforts to just Superbike. This allowed him to focus more completely on setting up his machine, but it deprived him of some extra track time. Tommy pitched in, giving his younger brother pointers he'd picked up on Saturday that Nicky could utilize on Sunday, and his insightful analyses were often quite helpful. "It was cool to watch him [in Superbike]," Tommy says.

With Kurtis Roberts and much of the AMA Superbike pack on his heels, Nicky heads down the Corkscrew at the 2002 Laguna Seca stop. Unfortunately, Eric Bostrom is already out of the frame, but Nicky's runner-up finish stockpiled more points toward a championship. (Tom Hnatiw)

BELOW: Never one to give up on a race without a fight, Nicky calls a corner worker to extinguish his burning RC51 in hopes of reentering the Pikes Peak Superbike feature. (Riles/Nelson)

RIGHT: Aboard a Honda RS750 leased from Terry Poovey, Nicky tucks in for the Springfield Mile's straightaway. He raced the event twice that year in hopes of notching an elusive Mile win, but could only muster a fourth and an eighth. (Flat Trak Fotos)

Today, Nicky's singed bodywork hangs on a wall in the Hayden garage, between fairings from Tommy's Kawasaki and Roger's Erion Honda. (Chris Jonnum)

"Part of me wanted to be out there racing, but it was a big year for him, and to be able to see it unfold and cheer him on was good."

While a Hayden road race triple was proving elusive, May of that 2002 season saw the brothers sweep the podium at the Springfield TT (as described in Chapter 1). That feat alone would be enough to make most people's season, but before Nicky had cleaned off the victory champagne, he was thinking about the next day. His TT victory had put him yet another step closer to the elusive Grand Slam, with a Mile win being the only remaining hurdle to clear. The way Nicky saw it, Sunday's Springfield Mile marked the perfect opportunity to achieve that goal.

Nicky was no longer with his former dirt track team TCR, and compared to his factory road race effort, his dirt track exploits were being done on a shoestring. Nicky convinced a fellow racer, veteran Terry Poovey, to let him lease his discontinued V-twin Honda RS750, a fast bike that was equipped with a "twingle" engine that altered the firing order to mimic the more tractable power delivery of a single-cylinder motor.

Harley-Davidson was dirt track's only remaining factory team, and their bikes had ruled the long tracks for years. Back in the mid-'80s, however, Bubba Shobert had taken three GNC titles for Honda, and Ricky Graham had taken a private RS750 out of mothballs in '93 for one last Japanese crown. In its day, the bike had been the weapon of choice at Springfield, and with some TLC from Nicky, it was more than capable of challenging the XR750s.

Unfortunately, a win was not in the cards, and neither was the Grand Slam (at least not yet). Nicky led for a while but finished just off the podium, proving that more than any other dirt track specialty, the Mile is an event at which one

must pay dues. Prior to that weekend, Nicky had never even sat on the Honda twin, and his main focus had been on his road racing endeavors, while the series regulars—guys like Chris Carr, Kevin Atherton, and Johnny Murphree (that night's top three)—were racing in the dirt week in and week out. Nonetheless, thanks to his success in the TT, Nicky still remembers the weekend as one of the best of his life.

He didn't get much time to savor it, as the road race season picked up again the next weekend at Pikes Peak. Nicky went winless in Colorado (on a weekend that saw him crash and his RC51 catch fire, while Tommy topped Supersport). Nicky crashed again at the following weekend's doubleheader in Elkhart Lake, Wisconsin, but he came out on top at Brainerd.

Next up was Independence Day weekend, for which Nicky had plans to return to Springfield to race the venue's popular Short Track Grand National. Coming into the event, he practiced all Friday morning at Sunset Downs, then showered and headed to a holiday family picnic for which Rose had required his attendance. After making an appearance, Nicky headed back to the house to spend the rest of the hot day working on bikes. "I remember my buddies all calling me up from a pool party, saying, 'Hey, where are you?' and I'm out there mounting tires," Nicky says.

Nicky would be riding his Honda CRF450R, and although the Haydens had proven that motocross bikes could win TT races, they had yet to do so on a flat track. The choice was sure to raise a few eyebrows. "The night before the race," Nicky says, "I was lying in bed, thinking, 'God, I hope I don't embarrass myself on a motocross bike!' "

Nicky got a bit of help at the track, as Sloppy Simmons and Roy Hart (Marlin's brother) met him in Springfield to lend a hand. Still, Nicky was cutting grooves in his own tires between races. He pulled off the win nonetheless, besting

Bryan Bigelow by just over a second. It was the first non-TT Grand National ever to be won by a motocross bike.

After the race, AMA dirt track manager Bruce Bober demanded that the bike's motor be torn down and inspected, to ensure that it wasn't a cheater. Of course the machine passed (the displacement limit for singles is 505cc, and the Honda was only a 450), but by the time Nicky got it back, it was just a bunch of parts in a box. Rather than try to put it back together by flashlight, Nicky paid a kid from the amateur AMA Grand Championships (which were run in Springfield that same weekend) to take the motor back to Honda in California for reassembly.

Two days after Nicky's Short Track win, the Haydens traveled to California for the World Superbike/AMA Superbike weekend at Mazda Raceway Laguna Seca. This U.S. round of the World Superbike series provided Nicky with an opportunity to try his first world championship event, as a wild card. It made for a busy weekend, though, as there were two World races plus the AMA racing. He managed a runner-up finish in the AMA Superbike race and finished a solid fourth in the first World SBK contest, but he crashed in the second World outing and took out series regular Noriyuki Haga. Meanwhile, Tommy celebrated his 24th birthday with a Superstock vic-

tory. Then Nicky returned to Illinois for the vaunted Peoria TT, where he tallied yet another dirt track win.

Throughout the dirt track season, the AMA continued to consistently order postrace teardowns on Nicky's CRF whenever he would show up to race. It even got to the point where the bike was inspected after the Tunica, Missouri, race—an indoor Short Track that was too short to enable cheater power to do any good, even if Nicky had had it! Once, after the engine had been disassembled, the AMA realized that their gauges weren't working and that they wouldn't be able to check the measurements. "I don't think some guys liked me coming in and beating the dirt track boys," Nicky says, "and I don't think Bruce Bober liked the idea of a part-time racer poaching his series."

Perhaps Nicky's detractors assumed he was getting factory dirt track assistance from Honda, but the truth was that he was ordering his own tires and fuel, and buying his own tools, parts, and pit equipment. Fahie would occasionally fly in a day or two before a race to fine-tune things, but other than that, Nicky was on his own. "Honestly," Nicky says, "I would load my bikes up myself and drive them to the track. By this time, I had seen how it was done right, and I enjoyed trying to do that on my own."

Nicky carried the momentum from Peoria into the next weekend's race at Mid-Ohio, where he won the second half of the Superbike doubleheader, just two days before his 21st birthday. To celebrate the occasion, Nicky threw a big, blowout party on Earl's Lane.

Despite the hectic race schedule, such bashes were actually a fairly regular occurrence that summer at the Owensboro compound. Many of the brothers' buddies had bought Honda XR100 play bikes, and the Haydens began holding nighttime mini "nationals" at Sunset Downs, where they'd turn on the floodlights and let everyone loose. Tommy, Nicky, and Roger

spent much of the time watching the action or helping Earl run the flags, although they did mix it up on occasion. Soon, a formal race format emerged, with heat races and a one-lap "Superpole" qualifying session. After it was all over, everyone would cool off in the Hayden pool.

"That was a lot of fun, because it was just the boys out there hanging out and going crazy," Nicky says. "A lot of the girlfriends started showing up, and then even more of our buddies started coming—the whole crew. I guess they weren't really parties, but it was a good time."

The weekend after his birthday celebration, Nicky returned to Springfield yet again, for the venue's second Short Track Grand National of the season. Once again, Nicky came out on top, giving him four dirt track victories on the year. (He would also win at the Formula USA–sanctioned postseason Del Mar Short Track.)

The week after his win, Nicky and his friends decided to make a trip to Bowling Green, a college city 70 miles south of Owensboro, in southern Kentucky. The original plan was to hire a limousine, but the group grew to the point where they wouldn't all fit. They decided to charter a bus, Nicky using his modest Springfield winnings to pay for half and the rest of the group teaming up to cover the remainder. "We got there, and we'd just pull up in front of bars or frat parties and invite all the girls into the bus," remembers Dano Legere, a good friend of the Haydens who was on the trip. "The next thing you know, it was like 12 of us guys, and something like 40 girls! We pretty much just pretended it was spring break for the night, seeing who had the most game with sorority girls. I think they're still talking about that night in Bowling Green!"

Coming into the road race series finale at VIR, the two older brothers were on form, and they pulled off a Hayden triple of sorts with Nicky winning the Saturday half of the

Superbike doubleheader (giving him a total of nine victories on the year) and Tommy nabbing victories in both of his classes. In the points chases, Tommy finished off the year second in both Supersport (33 points behind Aaron Yates) and Superstock (17 points behind Jimmy Moore). "If it weren't for that crash at Daytona, I think we'd have come really close to winning a championship," Lombardo says.

As for Nicky, VIR was where he wrapped up the AMA premier-class title, becoming the youngest Superbike Champion in history, with Bostrom taking second in points and Duhamel third; Mladin had an uncharacteristic off year and ended up seventh. "That was probably the best season of my life," Nicky says. "I was healthy and won a lot of races, and we had a lot of fun."

It had indeed been an incredible season: Victory at the Daytona 200, the Springfield podium sweep, the AMA Superbike title—even without the Grand Slam or a Hayden road race triple, it was the stuff of fairy tales.

Nicky had souvenirs made to commemorate the occasion: He ordered three custom rings—one for each of his parents and one for himself. The rings featured his No. 69 on the stone surrounded by the words *Superbike Championship,* *Hayden,* and *9 Races,* along with small pictures of Nicky and a checkered flag.

RIGHT: Earl joins Nicky on the start grid in 2004 at the Netherlands' history-rich Assen TT. Nicky had been on his own for much of his rookie season, but Earl has attended many of his races since then. (Andrew Northcott) FAR RIGHT: Under the watchful eye of Valentino Rossi, Nicky practices a start at the 2003 Le Mans Grand Prix. The two teammates weren't close friends, but they did respect each other, a relationship that has continued ever since. (Andrew Northcott)

CHAPTER 10 # BACK OVERSEAS

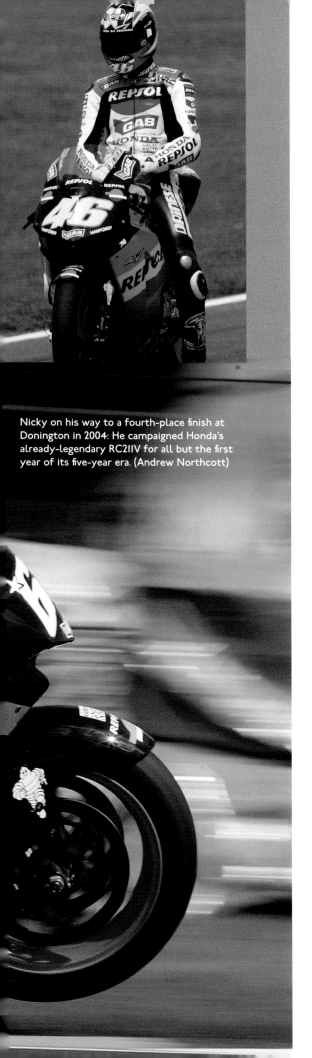

Nicky on his way to a fourth-place finish at Donington in 2004: He campaigned Honda's already-legendary RC2IIV for all but the first year of its five-year era. (Andrew Northcott)

Two hours after the 2002 AMA Superbike finale, Nicky wasn't toasting with champagne or reliving his drive to the title. Instead, he was sitting in a rental car in the Virginia International Raceway parking lot, discussing MotoGP options with Steve Dicterow and Gary Howard.

After his comment five months earlier about the 2002 Daytona 200 being Nicky's last, Dicterow set about making his prediction come true. He had traveled to the first MotoGP round in Suzuka, Japan, where he preached the gospel of his promising young rider to various team principals. As Nicky's success had mounted over the course of the season, he had drawn more and more interest from overseas, and by the time the 21-year-old wrapped up the title, International Racers had several options.

"Nicky wanted to race against the world's best," Dicterow says. "We felt like the younger he was when he got over there, the better off he'd be."

It was a huge challenge. The Grand Prix circuit is the top motorcycle-racing championship on the planet—Formula One on two wheels—with a history dating back to 1949. The champions' names—Mike Hailwood, Giacomo Agostini, Barry Sheene, and Americans like Kenny Roberts and Kevin Schwantz—are legendary and heroic.

Although Nicky was ready to change racing series, he preferred not to change manufacturers, and Dicterow made it clear during all of his negotiations that Honda was their first choice. That said, they wanted a factory motorcycle, and a factory Honda MotoGP spot is an enviable position indeed—much harder to come by, even, than a spot on American Honda's Superbike team. With riders like Freddie Spencer, Eddie Lawson, Wayne Gardner, and Mick Doohan, Honda had accumulated no fewer than 12 rider championships at that point. It's not hyperbole to say that Repsol Honda is the most prestigious team in motorcycle racing.

One of the spots on the two-rider team had already been spoken for, as Valentino Rossi—fresh off his second premier-class title in a row—had

LEFT: Nicky in action at the 2003 Suzuka 8 Hours: Note the rubber drinking hose running from a water bladder in the hump on his leathers to his helmet, enabling hydration in the race's typically sweltering conditions. Due to a lap-two crash, Nicky didn't get much opportunity to use it. (Andrew Northcott)
OPPOSITE: At the 2003 Suzuka 8 Hours, Nicky rolls his Seven Stars Honda superbike off the presentation stage to begin his one-lap qualifying session. No. 11 is reserved for the race's top team, which is what Nicky and Ryuichi Kiyonari were considered. (Andrew Northcott)

one more season remaining on his second two-year contract with Honda. Before signing with Honda for 2000, the charismatic Italian had ridden Aprilias to world championships in the two Grand Prix support classes—125cc and 250cc. He finished second to American Kenny Roberts Jr. in his rookie year in the 500cc class, then won that platform's final season in 2001. The same year that Nicky had taken his AMA crown, Grand Prix racing had initiated a two-year transition from 500cc two-strokes to 990cc four-strokes, and Rossi had ushered the new era in with yet another championship, winning 11 of 16 races along the way.

Honda's RC211V was the bike to beat in MotoGP, and the single open position with Repsol Honda—vacated by Tohru Ukawa—was a hot commodity. Superbike riders were considered desirable, as their experience on four-strokes would theoretically help them adapt more quickly to the new MotoGP machines than their two-stroke-bred European counterparts. The conventional wisdom was that the second Honda MotoGP seat would go to Texan Colin Edwards, who had just won his second World Superbike title for Honda that season and was also ready to make the move to the planet's top motorcycle racing championship.

On the other hand, Nicky's youth and his dirt track background were factors in his favor. The premier-class bikes' monstrous power meant that being comfortable with a sliding rear tire was a vital ability, and nothing taught that skill better than dirt track—as had been demonstrated by American heroes like Kenny Roberts, Wayne Rainey, and Lawson. "From

the mid-'80s to the mid-'90s," says Arai's Bruce Porter, "if you were an American involved in Grand Prix racing, there was a steel shoe hanging somewhere in your closet. That's just the way it worked."

Said heroes were still represented by International Racers and were in positions to potentially influence the Haydens. Roberts, who was now running his own Proton Team KR outfit, had kept track of the Hayden boys for many years, and would sometimes say to Earl, half-jokingly, "Tell me when you've got one ready." His team was already set, however (with Jeremy McWilliams and Nobuatsu Aoki), and, anyway, the proprietary KR bikes weren't competitive enough for Nicky to seriously consider.

Yamaha, on the other hand, was a player. The team had decided not to renew Max Biaggi's contract and was interested in teaming a young, emerging rider with veteran Carlos Checa. "We thought of Hayden, because he was a big talent," says Yamaha team manager Davide Brivio. "You could say he was the Valentino Rossi of the United States at that point—a great rider who was very popular, and who is nice and has a great personality. Wayne Rainey was a sort of advisor to Yamaha, and I remember that he had a high opinion of Nicky."

Yamaha asked Rainey to intervene on their behalf, prompting the three-time champ to interrupt a vacation at Lake Tahoe on the California-Nevada border and meet with Nicky, International Racers founder Gary Howard, and Yamaha representatives at his home in Monterey, just down the road from Mazda Raceway Laguna Seca. "Nicky was the top AMA guy," Rainey says, "and I knew if you could dominate the AMA series, you could do well in Europe. Nicky was doing that—he was the best guy in America."

Several teams showed interest, but the main contenders were Honda and Yamaha. Rainey was pushing for Yamaha, but the company was struggling. Rainey himself had won

Yamaha their most recent premier-class title, and that had been a decade ago—two years before Nicky and Tommy had ridden for him in the Open Ducados. Their new YZR-M1 four-stroke MotoGP bike had only won two events that season at the hands of Biaggi.

In terms of competitiveness—Nicky's primary concern—Honda's RC211V was much more desirable, and yet another hero was pushing Nicky that way. "I called him and told him how loyal Honda had been to me," says Bubba Shobert, Nicky's boyhood idol. "I said that if he went with them, he wouldn't regret it." Five-time champ Mick Doohan was also recommending that Nicky stay with Honda.

Honda, however, preferred that Nicky remain Stateside for one more season, urging him to defend his AMA Superbike title. With Rossi in place and Edwards presumably set to take Ukawa's place, both of their spots were spoken for, and although Honda said they would try to find a MotoGP seat for Nicky in 2004, they couldn't even guarantee that it would be a factory slot. If he stuck with the company, he might find himself on a private, satellite outfit, without access to the latest, updated parts. Still, it was tough to walk away from such a respected manufacturer. "I didn't want to be that fool that left Honda," Nicky says. "I'd been with them a long time, and I knew what they were capable of. I was going back and forth in my mind."

Gary Mathers, who had brought Nicky to American Honda but had recently left the company, had driven to the VIR finale from his house in North Carolina to watch Nicky wrap up the title. At that race, during a Clayton Foundation charity event that had some of the top riders stripping to their swim trunks onstage to raise money, he spoke with Earl, urging him to keep Nicky in America for one more year. "I always thought that if you won a championship, you should stay another year to defend it," Mathers says. "I didn't think he was ready, and I

thought he could use the experience." Gary Nixon thought he should stay for another year as well.

On the other hand, Nicky's own crew chief, Merlyn Plumlee, thought he should seize the opportunity. Not surprisingly, Nicky soon began second-guessing himself, sometimes wanting to make the move and other times wondering if he was ready to leave Kentucky and go overseas. Many are the young riders who have made marks in their realms and then advanced to the top class prematurely, only to disappear off the radar. "You hear some of these horror stories about dirty water, or about being in South Africa and seeing people get shot," Nicky says. "I was thinking, 'What if I leave Honda, sign a two-year deal, get over there, and decide that I hate it?'"

The negotiations reached their height during a Dunlop tire test at Daytona the week after the last race. During the day, Nicky was spinning laps around the Speedway's banks, and during the evenings, he was on the phone with his managers, representatives from Honda and Yamaha, translators, his sponsors, and his parents.

Nicky was leaning toward accepting Yamaha's offer and going to MotoGP, and the deadline for making a decision was nearing. "We wanted to stay with Honda," Dicterow says, "but we also wanted to go to MotoGP. When push came to shove, our decision was that getting him to MotoGP one year earlier mattered to us."

Shortly after the tire test, Dicterow called Nicky in Owensboro for a weighty conversation. As is usually the case when he's doing phone interviews with the media or making important business calls, Nicky was walking around on his family's tennis court with a cordless telephone. "Are you sure this is what you want to do?" Dicterow asked.

Nicky asked Dicterow for a few minutes to think. "That's a big decision," Nicky remembers. "It's not like, 'Do you want to eat at McDonald's or Hardy's?' This is, 'Are you going to

race superbikes for Honda, or pack up and go to Europe for MotoGP?'"

Really, though, Nicky knew what he wanted to do by this point, and it wasn't long before he called his manager back and told him he was ready: Dicterow could accept Yamaha's offer. "In the end, I decided that what I wanted my whole life was to be world champion, and this was my chance," Nicky says. "I might never get that opportunity again, and this was the only way to find out if I could do it. That's just the way I am—I'm always looking for the next goal, the next target. I saw everybody getting fast on these four-strokes, and I didn't want to give them any more time. I didn't want to wait until it was too late."

Dicterow called Yamaha to accept the offer, while Nicky— still under contract with Honda—packed his bags and headed for Chicago to make a required appearance at the company's annual September dealer show. There, he spoke with American Honda vice president Ray Blank, explaining that he had made his decision. To his amazement, the executive told him he'd see what he could do.

As is standard practice in rider contracts, Honda had first right of refusal, which meant they could keep Nicky if they offered equal money for an equal position—that is, a spot on their factory MotoGP team. Just when he thought the process was over, Nicky found himself back in discussions, Yamaha ringing him on his cell phone and Honda calling his hotel room. "I'd been thinking about the decision for weeks, and once I finally made it, it was almost like I had to go through it all again."

Their bluff called, Honda decided they had invested too much in Nicky, and with some pressure from the U.S. office, Honda Racing Corporation (HRC) told him they were prepared to offer him a two-year contract to ride the factory RC211V.

With the weight of the decision removed from his shoulders, Nicky was walking on air for the remainder of the dealer meeting. Roger was there as well, representing Erion Honda, and they took in a Cubs game at Wrigley Field with Erion rider Jake Zemke and their friend Eric Reynolds. Each morning, Nicky would train with Honda motocrossers Ricky Carmichael and Ernesto Fonseca.

Aware that his days of racing dirt track would be over when he went to MotoGP, Nicky and Roger flew from Chicago to Memphis on Friday night for an indoor AMA flat track race in Tunica, Missouri. Earl, Dan Fahie, and family friend Darrell "Tater Tot" Stallings had driven from Owensboro, and they met the brothers at the hotel. In the race, Nicky led early on, but a bump from Johnny Murphree put him on the ground and brought out a red flag. Forced to line up last in the single-file restart, Nicky nonetheless managed to work his way up to third by the finish. "That was one of my best races ever," Nicky remembers.

October's Formula USA Del Mar Short Track was Nicky's final chance to get another dirt track win before heading to MotoGP, and he put it to good use. With a group of motorcycling legends on hand, including daredevil Evel Knievel, Nicky grabbed the pole, leading the final wire-to-wire for the victory. "I'm just on hold," Nicky said to *Cycle News* reporter Scott Rousseau of his dirt track career. "I'm not done with it by any means. Some way, somehow, I'll be back in here somewhere. But this will be a good one to think about for the next couple of years."

Was there a blackout? A glance in the hall revealed that light was visible under the doors of the hotel rooms next to Nicky's, but for some reason, his wall switch didn't seem to work and the TV wouldn't turn on. He tried calling the front desk, but no one spoke English, so—bleary from his long

RIGHT: Nicky leads Aprilia rider Colin Edwards through a Suzuka corner during what was the debut Grand Prix for both Americans. Edwards ended up sixth, while Nicky was seventh. (Andrew Northcott)

Trainer Aldon Baker speaks with Nicky at the 2004 Dutch Grand Prix. Baker had earned a strong reputation working with motocrosser Ricky Carmichael. "Both riders are focused, and they give it 100 percent," Baker says. "They're in different genres, but they have an awful lot in common." (Andrew Northcott)

flight—Nicky finally gave up, showered in the dark, and went to bed.

Nicky was in Malaysia for Repsol Honda's first pre-season test at the Sepang Circuit, near Kuala Lumpur, and only the next morning did he learn that some overseas hotels require a room key be inserted into a slot on the wall in order for the electricity to work. On a trip to Honda headquarters not long after, Nicky went to bed one night wearing two pairs of socks and all his clothes, because he couldn't figure out how to turn on the heat in his Tokyo hotel room. Nicky obviously had a lot to learn, and the lessons weren't confined to hotel rooms.

The first Grand Prix of 2003—the first of Nicky's career—was in early April in Suzuka, Japan—the same track around which he and his brothers had made countless imaginary laps during their make-believe Suzuka 8 Hours in the Owensboro driveway. About three laps into his first Grand Prix Friday practice session, the throttle on Nicky's factory Honda stuck open. Approaching the famous Spoon Curve in fifth gear at 150 mph, Nicky had to jump off. "To this day, it was the fastest I've ever crashed in my life," he remembers.

When Nicky returned to the garage and told his team what had happened, the engineers reacted with incredulity: Not only had this rookie managed to total their mighty, million-dollar RC211V in just a few minutes, but—they seemed to be thinking—he also had the temerity to essentially blame *them* for the blunder?! Only later that night, after examining the information collected by the bike's onboard data acquisition system, did the technicians realize that debris had indeed worked its way into the throttle body, causing it to stick. Nicky was proven correct, but his initiation had been anything but seamless. "That really didn't help the way things started—to have that happen five minutes into my first GP," Nicky says, "and then have them think I was making up a story."

Despite Honda's enviable engineering reputation, HRC is almost as famous for its less-than-nurturing environment when it comes to its riders. "It's like, 'Here's the motorcycle; you ride it, and we don't want any input,'" says Mathers, who worked with the company for 16 years. "He went [overseas] earlier than I thought he should have, and with him being an American, I was worried that he might do poorly for six months and then they would turn on him."

The team's Suzuka problems continued on Saturday, as they sent Nicky into the first qualifying session a few minutes after it started, by which time it had begun to rain. Wet conditions continued, and by day's end, most riders' best times had come during the first few laps of the morning, when the track had been dry. As Nicky had put in no dry laps, he was mired in 22nd position on the start grid.

The race actually went relatively well for Nicky. He battled with Edwards—who had signed for the upstart Aprilia team when his Honda deal fell through—and finished seventh. The day was flawed by tragedy, however, as Gresini Honda rider Daijiro Kato suffered a fluke 125 mph crash into a wall near the final chicane, sustaining severe injuries to his head, neck, and chest. Two weeks later, the Japanese racer passed away.

Nicky again placed seventh at the next round in Welkom, South Africa—another respectable result on another unfamiliar circuit. He was learning quickly. "It was a big step, going from Road Atlanta and tracks I grew up on to racing against the best guys in the world, on tracks they knew and in their backyards," Nicky says.

If the racing was unfamiliar, life away from the track was even more foreign. In order to be near Honda's GP race shop in Aalst, Belgium, Nicky had tried to set up a temporary home away from home in a nearby Best Western hotel. He joined the local gym and bought a bicycle as a way to train after injuring his foot in one of two Friday crashes at the French Grand Prix, but his social life was pretty much nonexistent. "Not many people spoke English, and I pretty much hung out by myself there for quite a while," Nicky recalls.

It didn't take long for Nicky to discover that unlike the American race teams, the MotoGP squads really don't treat their race shops as home bases where they work between events. Instead, the mechanics work out of the team semis and in the circuit garages, then stay in their home countries during the breaks; only the truck driver and the parts manager spend much time in the shop.

Because of this, Nicky actually felt most at home when he was at the races. He was quickly becoming familiar with the MotoGP community, and because he had signed up for a service that delivered a motor home to every European round—complete with English-language satellite television—he didn't have to stay in hotels.

Nicky was also traveling to Japan quite frequently, as his contract required him to race in the Suzuka 8 Hours that summer. That, in turn, necessitated his attending several tests at the same circuit where Kato had lost his life during Nicky's debut Grand Prix.

Nicky's results dropped off a bit after the first two races, but at round 9, at Germany's Sachsenring, he notched his first top-five finish, putting him 10th in points. The series' traditional August break followed, but Nicky had to head back to Japan for the 8 Hours, in which he was teamed with Ryuichi Kiyonari to ride a Seven Stars tobacco–sponsored VTR1000 superbike. There, after two days of practice and qualifying in stifling heat and humidity, Nicky's race ended on the start of the second lap; another rider had blown his engine and dropped oil in the race's first turn, and oil flags were shown too late when the pack came around to begin lap 2. Suzuka's notoriously dangerous corner marshals were slow to wave caution flags, and Nicky was one of several riders to hit the oil and go down.

Nicky had always enjoyed summertime in Kentucky, and it was difficult for him to be away so much. "I remember calling home, and my family and friends would be hanging out together or be headed to Mid-Ohio like we used to do," Nicky says. "I wasn't exactly setting the world on fire in Grand Prix, so it was definitely hard."

"The biggest adjustment for me was that we were so many time zones apart," says Nicky's older sister, Jennifer. "It was difficult to call him sometimes, and I didn't always know what he was up to, like I did with my other brothers. I worried about him a little bit, because it wasn't that long after 9/11 had happened. He had always had such a support system with my brothers, and now he would deal with it over there on his own."

Nicky also missed the American races. He was no longer racing dirt track, which meant dreams like the Grand Slam and winning the Daytona Short Track and the Daytona 200 in the same weekend would most likely never become a reality. That year, the French Grand Prix coincided with Springfield weekend back in the States, and Nicky placed a call to race announcer Donny Bargmann. "We were getting ready to do the main, and a kid came up to me with a cell phone," Bargmann remembers. "I said, 'I can't talk; we're getting ready to do this race,' but he said I should take it. It was Nick, and I said, 'What are you doing, buddy?' He said, 'Well, I'm in Le Mans, and I heard Tommy made the main. I want to hear you call it.' I just sat the phone down, and he listened to me call the race."

"That first year, a lot changed for me," Nicky says. "I always used to go to the races with my brothers—that's just the way we did it since I was 3 years old. Tommy and I would always talk about stuff—braking markers, lines, and different things. I guess I didn't realize how tight I was with my brothers until that year."

Earl managed to attend some rounds when he wasn't hit-

Though he looks good testing the lean limits at the 2004 Catalunya Grand Prix, Nicky would later drop out with engine problems. Between that race and five others he crashed out of, 2004 gave Nicky the worst finishing record of his MotoGP career. (Andrew Northcott)

Nicky in 2003 MotoGP action on the RC2IIV—a step up from AMA Superbike in terms of both competition and performance. (Andrew Northcott)

ting AMA races to support Tommy and Roger, and Rose also came over for a couple, but it wasn't uncommon for Nicky to be on his own.

The press and some fans were giving Nicky a hard time, grumbling that the factory Honda spot should have gone to Edwards. "He was on the top team," says former American Grand Prix racer Randy Mamola, who now follows the series as a television commentator, "so of course there was a lot of outright jealousy, especially from Europeans. The class is so competitive, and he had Rossi alongside him. He was pretty wide-eyed, as you would imagine, but you could see that he was still aggressive."

As for being teamed with Rossi, Nicky enjoyed the experience, but he knew better than to expect too much help. "I looked at it as a big opportunity to try to learn from a guy who already had a handful of world titles," Nicky says, "but teammates in MotoGP aren't like a basketball team or something—it just means you have the same color bikes. He was always cool with me and straight up about everything, but it's not like he took me under his wing and tried to help me up to his speed as soon as possible. I would have thought less of him if he did. At times, it was nice with him winning all the time because I think it helped make the team expect and need less from me, but in other ways it was hard because there was so much extra attention and media focused on and around the team."

In fact, Nicky's results were improving. Back in Japan, four races after the summer break, he finished fourth in the Motegi Grand Prix, and when third-place finisher Makoto Tamada was disqualified for rough riding, Nicky ended up with his first top-three result. Unfortunately, the decision to penalize Tamada came too late for Nicky to take part in the podium celebration, but two races later, he notched his first "real" podium finish at Australia's Phillip Island—a rare MotoGP counterclockwise

track, more natural for a left-turning dirt tracker. When the 16-race series wrapped up in Valencia, Spain, in November, Nicky was a commendable fifth in the final points standings, with Rossi having taken his third premier-class title.

That first season reminded Roberts of when Nicky was racing his son Kurtis in AMA, where the legendary racer noticed him constantly working on establishing margins and learning what he could get away with. "It always worked out that Kurtis was faster in the beginning of the day on Friday, and then Nicky gradually worked his way up," Roberts says. "Pretty soon, Nicky was as quick as Kurtis if not quicker. It was the same way in 2003: At times, he was just struggling, but then by race day, he was better. A lot of guys—especially Americans—start out the race forward and then work their way backward. Nicky was the opposite."

Over the off-season, Nicky signed several new sponsorship deals, trading in Joe Rocket leathers for Alpinestars and picking up Oakley sunglasses and Red Bull energy drink. Nicky had actually been one of the first riders to wear an Alpinestars suit back in the late '90s, and the company was happy to have him back. "I'd gotten to know him better and better over the years," Alpinestars president Gabriele Mazzarolo says. "Even though he was with other companies, we remained friendly, and I believed that eventually he would be back with us. I didn't put any pressure on him, though; it was something that evolved naturally. I see him all the time, and he's an excellent person. He personifies what we want to stand for."

Fresh off his third premier-class title, Rossi—fed up with HRC focus on technology and ignoring their riders—had moved to Yamaha. He was replaced at Honda by journeyman Alex Barros, but Nicky's deal with Honda was for two years. Big things were expected of him for 2004.

In October 2003, Nicky and Tommy purchased a

condominium near Dan Fahie's place in Southern California, giving the mechanic and his family a break during their winter boot camps. "Dan was starting to have kids, and I was starting to feel a little bad now and then," Tommy says with a laugh. "It's one thing to come for a week, but there were three of us for two months every winter, all sleeping on air mattresses in one bedroom and rolling our suitcases into the hallway at night to have enough room." They bought the condo over the phone, site unseen, and Rose stayed with the brothers for a week to help them set it up, while they trained hard.

Another big change was the hiring of Aldon Baker as Nicky's personal trainer. A former bicycle racer from South Africa, Baker also worked with then-Honda-mounted motocross great Ricky Carmichael, who had introduced him to Nicky. "Ricky and I spoke, and we thought it was a good way to change stuff up," Baker says. "Also, it was good for the future, because we knew Ricky would be retiring in a couple of years. I'd always had a soft spot for road racing anyway, so it was good."

Baker visited the Hayden house, ran some tests on Nicky,

and developed a structured plan, with focus on improving strength and cardiovascular performance, as well as nutrition. In addition, he helped arrange a sponsorship for Nicky with Specialized bicycles.

For 2004, having consulted with Freddie Spencer, Nicky decided to mimic the three-time world champion's program of flying back to the States when there was a weekend off between races. That helped with the homesickness, and between Baker and Earl, Nicky now had someone with him at almost every race.

"Earl's the only guy who puts in more hours flying around with his kids than I do!" Roberts says. "When I go to an American race and I see him, I say, 'You go to every one of these.' He says, 'Every one!' That's unbelievable, the amount of mileage that guy has stacked on. He certainly gets on a lot of airplanes."

Still, Nicky's results suffered the sophomore jinx. He once again started with a pair of fifth places, in Welkom and Jerez, but then came an 11th in Le Mans, France, and a couple of DNFs at the Mugello circuit in Italy and the Circuit de Catalunya in Spain.

With MotoGP's transition to four-strokes complete, the manufacturers had put significant time and money into developing the big bikes, which were becoming much easier to control—a trend that would continue. As tire technology improved and electronic traction-control aids became more advanced, the bikes were staying in line better, and Nicky's unique abilities weren't being rewarded. "I don't think dirt track helped me like I thought it would," Nicky says. "Knowing how to slide the bike isn't as big an advantage as it used to be."

"Nicky asks quite a lot from the front tire," says Michelin's then–motorcycle racing manager Nicolas Goubert. "For the rear, he quite often needs hard tires, because he slides so

Nicky rails a turn on his CRF at Grange Motor Circuit, a popular kart track in Southern California. Riding Supermoto and motocross helps the Haydens keep their skills sharp, but not without introducing some additional risks. (Scott Hoffman)

Tommy and Roger make a rare Grand Prix appearance at the 2004 Valencia MotoGP finale. The three brothers enjoyed themselves despite having their rental car broken into at a local mall, necessitating a drive to Madrid to have their passports replaced. (Andrew Northcott)

much. He has a much different riding style than many other riders, and he puts a lot of strain on the tires—compared to them."

Nicky tallied two more podium finishes, in Brazil and Germany, but he broke his collarbone and tore knee ligaments in Italy while training at Supermoto (a pavement-dirt hybrid for motocross-based bikes). He had to undergo surgery to have a metal plate and seven screws installed on the fracture, which in turn forced him to sit out the Portuguese round.

He returned just two weeks after the injury to contest Japan's Motegi Grand Prix, but even with painkilling injections from MotoGP's Mobile Clinic doctor Claudio Costa, the knee was extremely painful. To literally add insult to injury, Loris Capirossi got out of control in the first turn, knocking several riders—including Nicky—out of the race.

Nicky bounced back with decent results in Qatar, Malaysia, and Australia, but at the season finale in Valencia, Spain (where NBA great Michael Jordan was attending his first MotoGP), he crashed out while fighting for a podium position. At year's end, Nicky was eighth, three spots worse than his rookie season (and with five Hondas ahead of him), while Rossi was champion yet again. Nicky was still winless two years into his MotoGP career, and the press was saying that he had gone to MotoGP too early.

Nicky was disappointed enough for himself, but he also felt the weight of the entire United States on his shoulders. "I felt some responsibility to help open that gate and keep them wanting to get some Americans [in MotoGP]," he says.

"MotoGP was a big step for Nicky," says Davide Brivio. "Even for a European, it would be difficult to pass from superbikes to MotoGP, because he might only know 30 or 40 percent of the tracks—but at least he would know

the atmosphere a little bit. Nicky had to make a complete jump—from superbikes to Grand Prix bikes, plus to tracks that were totally unknown to him, and to a foreign environment. He didn't know anyone, and it was a really big step."

Still, Nicky had shown enough promise that he was being approached by other teams—including, once again, Yamaha, who had decided to part ways with Checa. In the end, though, Repsol Honda re-upped his contract. Nicky had retained his prized spot on the top factory squad, but his new teammate was Biaggi, a four-time 250cc world champion and the same rider Nicky had been in awe of when he visited the 1994 USGP as a spectator. Nicky knew he had to perform.

CHAPTER 11

BROTHERS AND TEAMMATES

At the second round of the 2004 season in Fontana, California, new teammates Tommy and Roger fight over the lead in the Supersport race. Tommy would take the win, but Roger could smell his first AMA victory. (Riles/Nelson)

LEFT: After 17 laps, Roger just nips Tommy at the Barber finish line to take his very first AMA road race victory. "Not only was it my first win, but it was a dream race," Roger says. "It's hard to beat a dogfight and a last-corner pass." (Riles/Nelson)
BELOW: Following one of the most animated victory laps those on hand could remember, Roger brings the checkered flag back down pit lane in Birmingham. Combined with a podium finish in Superstock, his debut AMA road race win in Supersport signaled to the world that he was a contender. (Riles/Nelson)

As Tommy pulled off his still-sweaty leathers in the Kawasaki team semi following the last Superstock race of the 2003 season, so great was his disappointment that just getting his head around it was difficult. Birmingham, Alabama's brand-new Barber Motorsports Park was hosting its first-ever AMA Superbike weekend, and although Tommy had just won the race—his fifth win in the class for the year—he had once again lost the title, this time to Josh Hayes. He was beginning to wonder if he was cursed and if he would ever land an AMA championship.

This one had been so close he could taste it. Tommy had won the first three rounds and led the points for the first half of the season, but a postrace tech inspection at California Speedway had found his ZX-6RR to have an illegally modified head. As a result, Tommy was docked 20 points and penalized $2,000, and by the time the series headed to the Barber finale, Hayes led by eight points. Despite Tommy's victory, Hayes took home the title, but without that penalty, and with all other things being equal, Tommy would have been Superstock champ.

"It was definitely a heartbreaker for me," Tommy says. "My team made a mistake, but there's not much else you can say—you win together and you lose together. The guys were just trying their hardest, and they definitely didn't do anything deliberate."

The stock classes strictly curb modifications to engines and suspension, and the top teams must tune their bikes right up to the limit—sometimes past it. The word "cheating" would be overstating it, though, as the modification had been limited to minor machining in the combustion chamber; if a team were to roll the dice on not getting caught, they'd be more likely to try something that would provide a bigger advantage, like overboring their cylinders. "We definitely felt like it was a gray area," Tommy explains. "Knowing they're going to check the heads first thing, that's not something you're going to try to squeeze by. No factory team's going to cross their fingers and hope they don't get caught."

Meanwhile, Tommy's Supersport chances had been hurt by a similar penalty at Road America, where he was docked 20 points for an illegal

BELOW LEFT: In addition to Supersport, Roger and Tommy both raced Kawasaki's new ZX-IOR in Superstock in 2004. Shown here entering the front straight at Laguna Seca, Roger didn't score a win, but he did finish the year sixth in points. (Riles/Nelson) **OPPOSITE:** Dan Fahie councils his new rider before he leaves pit lane at the 2004 Pikes Peak national. A longtime Hayden family friend, Fahie was already very familiar to Roger, and the crew chief's influence was just what he needed to step up his game. (Riles/Nelson)

oil pump. He had finished the year second in Superstock and third in Supersport, but with his résumé still lacking a national title, the critics were doubting whether he had what it takes. Tommy's consistency has never been questioned—his teams sometimes joke that he has forgotten how to crash—but some were beginning to wonder if he was simply too careful.

Even Tommy was beginning to second-guess himself. He looked back over the years, trying to identify what had gone wrong, thinking of where things could have gone better and of races where he may have left something on the table. He decided that for 2004, he would make absolutely sure that if he didn't win a title, it would not be due to a lack of trying with everything he had. "I made a conscious decision," Tommy says, "to put every last tenth of a percent that I could find into everything—riding, testing, training. Every day, I tried to look for just the smallest little bit extra that I could find."

His team and crew were behind him as well. Frustrated by what they saw as a moving target in the AMA Superbike regulations, Kawasaki was considering withdrawing from the

premier class, making success by Tommy in the stock classes all the more important. "My goal from the beginning was that I really wanted to be a part of his first national championship," says Joey Lombardo, then Tommy's crew chief.

Meanwhile, Roger was also suffering a dip in self-confidence. In 2002, when he and Nicky had both ridden for Honda teams, they had traveled together to races, tests, and sponsor commitments. Following Nicky's departure to MotoGP, however, the youngest Hayden brother had felt alone at Erion Honda, finishing the 2003 season 8th in Supersport and 10th in Formula Xtreme. His bikes were breaking down, and there was friction between him and team owner Kevin Erion. "Instead of going up, I was dropping off," Roger says. "I thought maybe I picked the wrong sport or something."

With a dearth of offers from good teams for 2004, and an unwillingness to settle for a mediocre squad, the 20-year-old—who still calls this period the "low of lows"—was considering ending his career prematurely. Fortunately, Attack Racing stepped in with an offer. The Richard Stanboli–owned outfit had earned success as a Suzuki satellite team, and for 2004 they were switching to Kawasakis, which meant Roger would be sharing test time with brother Tommy.

As the season approached, however, it began to appear that they might even be sharing a team truck. After Kawasaki finalized their decision to withdraw from AMA Superbike, Tommy's teammate, Eric Bostrom, asked to be released from his contract. He was let go to Ducati Austin just before December's big Daytona tire test, leaving an open spot on the factory team.

Kawasaki had a couple of options, but a card in Roger's favor was Dan Fahie, who had moved from Honda to Kawasaki in 2003 to work as Bostrom's crew chief. Fahie cast his vote for picking up Roger from Attack. He had a strong relationship with the Haydens, and Roger's having already familiarized

BELOW: Earl and Rose enjoyed seeing their oldest and youngest sons teamed together at Kawasaki, and not only because it made it easy for Earl to choose what color shirts to wear to the races. (Riles/Nelson)

RIGHT: Announcer Ben Cheatwood interviews Tommy on one of the many podiums he shared with Roger over the 2004 season. The brothers grew even closer as a result of their three years being teamed together at Kawasaki. (Riles/Nelson)

There's no "I" missing from that "56.7" on Roger's pit board at Pikes Peak. The Colorado track is now absent from the AMA schedule, but all three Hayden brothers—whose dirt track background made them comfortable on its short, counterclockwise layout—scored wins there. (Riles/Nelson)

himself with the Kawasaki over the off-season would theoretically make a potential transition smoother. Team manager Mike Preston decided it made sense, and he signed Roger to race Supersport and Superstock for two years. "I think that says a lot about Mike," Roger says. "I hadn't really done much to that point to deserve a factory ride, but he decided to take a chance. It changed my whole life."

Having a team that wanted him was just the type of environment that Roger needed, especially with Fahie as his crew chief. He finally got a chance to try out a factory bike, and although he wasn't hugely impressed the first time out, Fahie patiently explained that this would change. "I told him, 'Well, no, Rog, our bikes are pretty much like everybody else's—they're just bikes,'" Fahie says. "'The difference is that we make ours just for *you*. If you want the foot pegs that much lower, we're going to do it—but you have to be able to communicate that point.'"

That communication wasn't immediate. Roger has a focused nature that's belied by his laid-back exterior, and although he isn't exactly shy, he is reserved. At Kawasaki, he had to learn that although intensity is important on Sunday morning, it must be put away at times in the interest of better communication with the crew. If the lap times aren't coming, it's important to figure out why rather than get angry. This is an area where Nicky has always excelled.

With Fahie's help, Roger was learning quickly, and the crew was responding. "If everybody in our little clique *believes*, then he'll believe," Fahie explains. "And if *he* believes, then everyone in the clique believes—it just snowballs."

With the crewmembers going out of their way to feed Roger information and make him better, he learned more during his first several tests with Kawasaki than he had through his entire career up until then. "I was always a guy who would just ride it," he says, "but Dan always wants to think things out.

He's shown me the importance of sitting down and thinking about stuff and communicating. Coming from where I was, it was just the difference between daylight and darkness."

Among pundits, there was speculation on what life in the Kawasaki truck would be like with two brothers as teammates. The entire Hayden family is famous for its unity, but working together often introduces new and damaging stresses into relationships. Would Tommy's careful, methodical personality mesh well with Roger's more impulsive nature? "There were concerns," admits International Racers' Steven Dicterow.

"Tommy and Roger are about as different as two individuals can be," sister Jennifer confirms. "I was so excited for them to be together, because I thought there was a chance that it would be good for them—that they could learn from each other's differences. At the same time, I was a little bit worried that they would be too close to each other, being on the same team."

Coming into the 2004 season, Tommy and Roger were both on their games. They'd had a productive winter boot camp while staying with Nicky in their California condominium, and they were physically and mentally strong. Roger was visibly fitter by springtime, while Tommy had a new attitude that he felt might just give him the edge he needed to finally land that first title. "I felt like I needed to be a little more assertive—keep my consistency, but step it up a little and win a few more races," he says.

At the always-unpredictable Daytona opener, Tommy rode to patient third-place finishes, in both Superstock and Supersport, before notching a win in the Supersport class at California Speedway's round two on April 4, where he was seventh in Superstock. It was already clear that he was the class of the 600cc field, and that his main competition would be coming from Roger, who beat him by one position in both the Daytona Supersport contest (after leading for much of

[147]

Joey Lombardo talks lap times and setup with Tommy in 2004. Thanks to a youth spent helping to maintain the family's bikes, Tommy is an extremely technically savvy rider. (Riles/Nelson)

the race) and the Fontana Superstock event. The Daytona podium, in particular, had Roger fired up. "My whole mentality changed after that," he says. "I think it just made me a lot hungrier."

So far, the scenario was working fine. Especially early on, Tommy helped Roger with gearing choices or in choosing a tire. He and Fahie both encouraged Roger to think about what he was doing and why, and while the youngest Hayden brother was catching on quickly, he could always ask "What's Tommy using?" when he had a doubt. And Tommy knew that if he asked Roger's opinion on something, he could be 100 percent sure that he was getting a completely honest answer.

"Tommy's a great teacher, and Roger's a great student," Dicterow says. "They understood that Tommy had more experience than Roger, and that Roger could learn from Tommy. Roger's got all the talent in the world, but being around Tommy has made him progress even faster."

Sometimes one brother would even allow the other to draft behind him during qualifying, to set a better time. All bets were off during the races, of course, but even then, the natural desire to beat one's sibling means that sometimes if one brother is fast, the other one will pick up the pace.

There were also practical advantages. The brothers shared identical schedules, and they could communicate about setup and such whenever the subject came up—like in a rental car, on an airplane, or even around Rose's dinner table—rather than having to save questions for team meetings or pick up a telephone. It's

important to feel at home on a team, and if Tommy and Roger didn't feel at home on Team Kawasaki, they never would.

"Most teams aren't really *teams*," Fahie says. "In other trucks, there are independent units that wear the same color shirts. The information and knowledge is never passed on at the ground level. With Roger and Tommy, it wasn't like that—it was an honest-to-God team."

Meanwhile, Nicky was sometimes absent from his brothers' lives for weeks at a time during his lengthy overseas stints. The trio had been accustomed to eating, traveling, and working together, and although Rose and especially Earl did a good job of accompanying Nicky at most of his MotoGP races, Tommy and Roger were busy with their AMA duties. "It was a little different with us being at one race, and him being in another country at another race," Tommy says. "You try to keep up with it and follow it, but you don't know exactly what's going on."

Daily e-mails and instant messages helped, as did telephone conversations every few days. Tommy and Roger could record and watch Nicky's races on TV, and they enjoyed having a brother in the planet's top road racing series. "I'm a fan of the sport," Tommy says, "and any time you actually have a connection, that just makes it more interesting. You follow it closer and want to know everything about it."

It wasn't as easy for Nicky, however. The AMA rounds weren't broadcast in many non-U.S. countries, and it wasn't uncommon for Nicky and Earl to wake up in the middle of the night to watch the live timing on the AMA's website, cheering Tommy and Roger on through the laptop computer. It was a bittersweet experience. "I was happy for them to be doing so well," Nicky says, "but man, I would wish I was doing better in my racing, so we could all have a good Sunday."

During the third AMA round at Infineon Raceway in California's wine country, Tommy notched another Supersport

Sporting his signature orange highlights and a new Troy Lee paint job on his helmet, Tommy Gun drops into Laguna Seca's famous Corkscrew corner. (Riles/Nelson)

podium and was just off the Superstock box, while Roger had an off weekend. Then Roger shocked everyone at Barber's round four, where he, Tommy, and Yamaha riders Aaron Gobert and Jamie Hacking were involved in a race-long Supersport dogfight. Roger put a last-corner pass on Tommy to lead his big brother across the line by just three-hundredths of a second, scoring the first AMA win of his career and putting on a huge, animated victory celebration on the cool-down lap. Both brothers made the Superstock podium as well.

"It was awesome—one of the best days of my life," Roger says. "Not only was it my first win, it was a dream race. I wanted to prove some people wrong—people who said I would never win. That's not really the way you're supposed to look at it, but it definitely made me smile a little bit."

The day was also exceptional for Fahie. "Wow," he says. "There are a lot of special wins in my career, but that is a high-light, for sure. If he was racing with anyone else, it wouldn't have been nearly as big, but beating Tommy was big for him."

The win definitely made fans and people in the paddock take Roger more seriously. Suddenly, he wasn't just Tommy and Nicky's little brother, but a serious contender in his own right. "People always ask me, 'Who do you think is better, Tommy or Nicky?'" says legendary racer Gary Nixon. "I'll say, 'Boy, you better watch out—Roger's been taking their crap for 12 or 13 years; he's badass!'"

If Tommy wasn't already inspired to push his limits, being bested by Roger may have been just what he needed. He had already been beaten by Nicky in the 1999 Supersport title fight, and family unity notwithstanding, he didn't want it to happen again with Roger. "If Roger goes fast, then Tommy's going to go fast—for sure!" Fahie says. "Bike be damned, it doesn't make any difference: 'That's my little brother, who can't ride as good as I can. And I *know* he can't!'"

The week after Roger's win, Tommy bounced back with a Supersport victory at Fountain, Colorado's Pikes Peak International Raceway, and the win inspired a streak. He topped both classes at Road America in Elkhart Lake, Wisconsin, and followed with a Supersport victory at Brainerd and a Superstock win at Mazda Raceway Laguna Seca. With three rounds remaining, he had a 13-point lead on Roger in Supersport, and the next-closest racer was a further 51 points back.

Tommy went into conservation mode at that point, scoring two non-podium finishes, while Roger went on a tear with Supersport victories at Laguna, Mid-Ohio, and Road Atlanta. The long-awaited title went to Tommy, however, as he sewed it up with a safe sixth-place finish at the Virginia International Raceway finale. Roger was second, 352-343, and Tommy and Roger were third and sixth in Superstock, respectively.

"It was like getting a gorilla off my back," Tommy says of his first title. "It was just a huge relief for me. It seemed like I'd put so much thought, effort, and time into [my career]. There were a lot of ups and a lot of downs—letting titles slip away for whatever reason—and I finally showed I could do it."

The championship was also Lombardo's first as a crew chief. "From the outside, you can see that one son's path has gone a little bit straighter than the others," he says, comparing Nicky to his brothers. "The others have had more hurdles. I always believed in Tommy and thought it was going to happen, but after two years of coming close, it was a relief."

Important for the Haydens, the relationship between Tommy and Roger survived unscathed, perhaps even ben-efiting from the competition. They raced each other hard all season, but then they'd come back to the truck and talk about setup. Because they were brothers, they pushed one another to improve, and besides, there's nothing like keeping the win bonuses in the family. "In the end," says sister Jenny, "I think it was the best thing that could have happened to either one of them."

GRAND PRIX

Raceway

Seca 200

CHAPTER 12 USGP

LEFT: With the laps ticking down, Nicky takes to Laguna's front straight, his debut MotoGP victory within sight. "It's all kind of a blur," Nicky says, "[but] one thing I do remember is being relieved. Being at home and doing well on Friday and Saturday, I was supposed to win that race." (Andrew Northcott)

BELOW: For the first time in his MotoGP career, Nicky lines up in pole position. "The last couple of years have been frustrating when you're used to winning and getting poles," he had said in the post-qualifying press conference. "It feels good to be up front again." (Riles/Nelson)

OPPOSITE: On the Laguna Seca podium, Nicky pops the cork on the winner's champagne for the first time in his Grand Prix career. Having tasted victory in AMA Superbike, it had been tough to go two years in MotoGP without a win, so the Red Bull USGP was a relief. (Andrew Northcott)

Nicky wasn't really sure what to think as he sat in a folding chair at New York City's Rockefeller Plaza, with Philadelphia Eagles linebacker Dhani Jones and country music singer Keith Anderson just to his right. Along with celebrities like Tom Cruise, Brad Pitt, and Colin Farrell, Nicky had just been named to *People* magazine's "50 Hottest Bachelors of 2005" list, and the *Today* show was holding a mock version of "The Dating Game" in which Nicky, Jones, and Anderson competed for the heart of a 25-year-old blonde named Sara Hostetter.

As Al Roker hosted, Hostetter grilled the "contestants," and although Jones and Anderson held their own, they had to know they were doomed when she asked, "What's the fastest you've ever gone?" Upon hearing Nicky's "215 mph," Hostetter's mind was made up: "I don't know if my mom's going to be too happy about this," she said, "but I love a man who can ride fast."

After receiving a kiss from Hostetter and presenting her with an Alpinestars jacket, Nicky headed to a reception at *People*'s offices, where reporter Danielle Dubin said of him, "He really met all the criteria that we have for a hot guy—namely, that he's hot." Then came an autograph signing in the Time-Life Building lobby and an interview with *Inside Edition*.

It was June 15, 2005, and the mainstream press blitz was part of a publicity push for the upcoming Red Bull United States Grand Prix at Mazda Raceway Laguna Seca. The United States had hosted eight other Grand Prix rounds in the past, but the last time had been 11 years earlier, when Tommy and Nicky had attended the '94 USGP with sponsor Cliff Sherlock. The historic Laguna track had hosted all but the first two USGPs (which were held at Daytona in the '60s), and its return to Grand Prix glory was a major occasion. The old event had enjoyed victories by legendary American heroes like Eddie Lawson, John Kocinski, and especially Wayne Rainey, and although Nicky still had yet to win a MotoGP race, he was the United States' best hope in the July event.

Putting downtime during a 2005 test to good use, Tommy logs some time on a stationary bicycle. The brothers' training regimen is very specialized and highly disciplined. (Riles/Nelson)

After Nicky's re-signing with Honda at the end of 2004, the team had replaced much of his crew, including trading Trevor Morris for Pete Benson as crew chief. It was the New Zealander's first time in the position, but he had experience working with Valentino Rossi and, more important, he had Nicky's confidence.

"The first couple years he was in MotoGP, that chemistry didn't happen," says Merlyn Plumlee, the chief of Nicky's stellar crew at American Honda. "I could tell by his e-mails that he wasn't real happy—not that the guys he was with were bad, but it just wasn't the right mix for him. At one point, we even considered my trying to get over there, but I don't think that would have been good, because (a) I didn't have any MotoGP experience, and (b) he had moved on; he needed different stuff than what I had to offer. Anyway, I think that's when he realized how important that chemistry is, and he tries to cultivate it."

It's a trait shared by many great champions, including Rossi and Formula One hero Michael Schumacher, and the harmony it enables is worth any temporary discomfort required (such as the awkward vibe felt when Morris's crew had learned about the change four rounds from the end of the 2004 season). "We weren't really on the same page and weren't working well together," Nicky says of his previous crew. "You've got to be able to believe in your boys, and they've got to be able to believe in you and read the rider to get the most out of you. It wasn't anybody's fault."

In addition, International Racers had added Englishman Phil Baker as an agent, allowing more personal attention to and promotion of Nicky. One of Baker's first moves was to start an official relationship with the Make-A-Wish Foundation (which grants the wishes of children with life-threatening medical conditions) and to make special, orange wristbands molded with Nicky's "Chasin' a Dream" motto, to raise money for the charity.

Meanwhile, Nicky's year-old partnership with trainer Aldon Baker was really paying dividends. "The longer you're with an athlete, the more you can see a pattern develop in his training and fitness, and that's key," explains Baker, who by now was visiting Nicky in Kentucky on a regular basis and even traveling with him to races quite often. The two were in telephone contact daily, and Nicky could plug his heart-rate monitor into his laptop and e-mail training data for Baker to evaluate. Because Aldon was able to provide analytical proof of Nicky's improvement—through heart-rate information and lactic-acid testing—the rider's confidence began increasing as well.

LEFT: Nicky signs autographs in the Honda tent at Laguna Seca in 2005. Even before he became champion, Nicky's time was always in high demand at the Red Bull USGP. (Andrew Northcott)

"I know my plan's not easy," Baker says. "Athletes always say they'll do what it takes, but only a few of them will. People see the glory side of the sport, but there's an ugly side as well. I look for the guy that I know is committed—that has heart and discipline and that never says 'die.' Nicky is that guy."

By now, Tommy and Roger were also both working with Aldon, and after celebrating the holidays and attending Jennifer's graduation from nursing school, the three brothers started their California boot camp together in preparation for the 2005 season. Unfortunately, one particular training session did more harm than good.

The three brothers were riding their road bicycles together on Jamboree Road, heading downhill at about 35 mph, when they came upon a piece of metal pipe that had fallen off of a construction truck. Tommy darted to the left, Nicky to the right, and Roger, riding close behind, went straight into it and hit the ground hard. The results weren't pretty.

"I got up and just started running because it was so hot," Roger says. "I was kind of in shock. I've crashed a lot of times on motorcycles, but this one on a bicycle spooked me a little bit." When Roger gathered his wits and stopped running, he looked down to see road rash all over his body and a tendon literally hanging out of his knee.

While Roger waited roadside, holding his ripped Lycra bicycle shorts together with his hands, Tommy rode home to get their truck, while Nicky went on to finish the ride! "There was no need for both of them to help me," Roger says, "and Nicky said he needed to get in some more training. The season was about to start, and the clock was running!"

Tommy picked Roger up to take him to the hospital, but the first outpatient facility was closed. They finally found a clinic that would see Roger, and the nurses gave him so much medication that he was giggling as they cleaned the asphalt out of his knee and sewed it shut from the inside out. "The funny thing

was," Roger says, "Tom has a weak stomach, so for a while they thought they were going to have to give him the table."

The wound took months to heal and put a hitch in Roger's training plans, but he struggled along as well as he could, regularly visiting Dan Fahie's wife, Maria—a veterinarian—to have his bandages changed. With some help from Tommy in suiting up, Roger was able to ride by the time the first AMA round in Daytona rolled around, but he was in pain and struggled to 21-11 finishes in Supersport and Superstock, respectively. Meanwhile, Tommy won the Supersport race and finished seventh on the 1000.

With confidence gained from his 2004 championship, Tommy went on a tear through the first half of the season, finishing either first or second in the first six Supersport rounds, while Roger won at Pikes Peak and scored three other podium finishes. Both brothers were struggling in Superstock, with Tommy's Barber win and Pikes third being the only early bright spots. Still, Tommy and Roger held the top two spots in the 600cc class as the series headed into Laguna for the Red Bull USGP, where the AMA series would be racing as support classes to the MotoGP contest.

[157]

This would make the Laguna race a sort of reunion for the Hayden brothers, as all three would be racing at the same event. Nicky had struggled through a disappointing first half of his MotoGP season, crashing out of the opener in Jerez and failing to find the podium through the first seven rounds. The relationship with teammate Max Biaggi was rough, with the Italian having knocked Nicky off his bike on pit lane during the pre-season test in Malaysia, where he exited the Repsol Honda garage at high speed just as Nicky was pulling in. Nicky may have been a Hot Bachelor in *People*'s eyes as he headed to California, but he was only seventh in points, prompting him to joke to *Cycle News*' Henny Ray Abrams after getting his kiss on the *Today* show, "I finally won something this year!"

Built in 1957 by struggling Salinas architect Wallace Holm, Mazda Raceway Laguna Seca is situated on what used to be Fort Ord land in a valley just east of Monterey, California. A true old-school circuit that wasn't designed on a computer, like most modern tracks, the 2.238-mile ribbon of asphalt takes full advantage of the valley's natural terrain, twisting past its namesake lagoon and around the surrounding hillsides. It offers racers everything from its daunting turn one (in which riders crest a sharp rise at top speed while banked to the left) to its bus-stop final corner (a first-gear left that dumps onto the front straightaway), but its crown jewel is without a doubt the harrowing Corkscrew—a twisting, roller-coaster-like drop of more than 900 feet down a 30 percent grade. With the longest straightaway being just 0.6 miles long, the only thing the track lacks is a place for riders to catch their breath.

As the second-oldest circuit on the MotoGP schedule, Laguna presented concerns about whether it would be up to par for modern, faster Grand Prix machines. Since the '94 race, the Fédération Internationale de Motocyclisme (FIM,

the international sanctioning body) had instituted stricter safety criteria for MotoGP homologation, standards that Laguna didn't meet (although the track did host World and AMA Superbike races). In 1974, the land on which the facility sits had been given by the U.S. Military to the Monterey County Parks Department, and the non-profit group that operated it (the Sports Car Racing Association of the Monterey Peninsula, or SCRAMP) lacked the funds to make the necessary changes.

Fortunately, event sponsor Yamaha stepped in with $2 million in improvements—most of which involved expanding runoff areas on the outsides of corners to provide escape routes for out-of-control or crashing riders—and the FIM Safety Commission gave the track its stamp of approval less than a month before the scheduled race date.

If Nicky wanted to turn his season around, this was the place to do it. For a change, the MotoGP series was racing at a circuit that he knew better than his European competition, a track where he had scored wins in AMA Superbike and Superstock. When riders like Rossi and Marco Melandri began expressing their dissatisfaction with the track's safety even before turning a wheel, Nicky and fellow Americans Colin Edwards, John Hopkins, and Kenny Roberts Jr. knew they also had a mental advantage.

Nicky was accustomed to America's typically dangerous road race and flat track circuits, and whereas most European tracks run in a generally clockwise direction, Laguna has seven left turns and just four right—perfect for a former dirt tracker. In fact, the venue has always been kind to flat trackers, including Doug Chandler, Ben and Eric Bostrom, and of course Rainey, who lives just over the hill and even has one of the turns named after him. Thanks to his skills in motocross and TT, Nicky was comfortable with Laguna's flowing nature—that can penalize a mistake for several turns—and

BELOW: Nicky cuts loose on the podium with Colin Edwards and Rossi. "I've cried after losing before," Nicky says, "but that was the first time I cried over winning." (Riles/Nelson)

RED
U.S. GR
Mazda Rad
Laguna Sec

LEFT: Basking in the adulation of his home fans (including actor Matt LeBlanc, right), Nicky savors the moment during a post-race party in the Red Bull Energy Center. (Andrew Northcott)

with its extreme undulations (in qualifying, the bikes' data acquisition systems revealed that both wheels were leaving the ground in turn one and at the top of the Corkscrew). Best of all, Nicky and Edwards—now riding with Rossi on Yamaha's factory team—knew a "secret" line around some bumps at the bottom of the Corkscrew.

Nicky certainly wasn't lacking moral support at Laguna. On Thursday, he began running into old friends from his AMA days, and the entire Hayden family was on hand (relieved to finally be attending a single race at which all three brothers would be competing). There was a sellout three-day crowd of 153,653 attendees, and Red Bull's promotional efforts had helped draw celebrities including Brad Pitt, Matt LeBlanc, and Oscar winner Adrien Brody—not to mention Michael Jordan, who by now owned a Suzuki team in the AMA series. In addition, director Mark Neale was there with a crew, filming footage for a documentary on the race. With all of this attention came extra pressure for Nicky, who knew that his many fans would be content with nothing less than his premier MotoGP victory.

Though Nicky knew the track, it had been three years since he had ridden it, and he was a bit rusty in Friday's first, extended practice session. "When I first got there on a MotoGP bike, it just looked so different from what I remembered," Nicky says in *The Doctor, the Tornado & the Kentucky Kid* (*DTK*, the film eventually made by Neale). "All the lines and the straightaways felt so much shorter, and everything was happening faster."

Nicky got up to speed quickly enough, however, finishing the outing second-fastest to Camel Honda's Troy Bayliss, who had ridden at Laguna in the previous season's World Superbike race. Using a new, wide-profile Michelin front tire, Nicky topped all comers in that afternoon's practice.

Meanwhile, the Europeans and Japanese—the majority of whom had never ridden the track before—were struggling for

the most part. Melandri began a series of crashes that would last throughout the weekend, and Rossi was 6th- and 10th-fastest in the day's sessions.

Saturday morning saw Nicky once again at the top of the charts, turning a fast lap of 1'23.718". Later that day, in the all-important qualifying session, he grabbed the first MotoGP pole position of his career, with a time of 1'22.670"—the fastest lap ever around Laguna. Sharing the front row with him were Rossi (seven spots ahead of the next-fastest Laguna rookie) and veteran Alex Barros, who had raced at the last USGP over a decade earlier.

"It's a great feeling after all these years to be first when it counts," Nicky said in the press conference afterward. "The weekend just keeps getting better and better, and I just hope it keeps going in that direction . . . It's great to give all my people something to cheer about."

The other Hayden brothers also had reason to hope for strong results at Laguna. Tommy had two wins each in Supersport and Superstock at the facility, and Roger had won the previous year's Supersport contest. In addition, both brothers had snared their first AMA podiums at the track (Tommy in '97 in 600cc Supersport, Roger in 2000 in 750cc Supersport). In fact, the Red Bull USGP represented a rare opportunity for all three brothers to get podiums or even wins at the same event.

The trend continued on Sunday morning, with Nicky posting the top time in the MotoGP warm-up session, and Tommy grabbing pole during Supersport qualifying, two spots ahead of Roger. Shortly thereafter, however, the chances for triple success by the Haydens took a big hit: As Nicky stayed loose on his stationary bicycle in the motor home, Tommy led the Superstock race until two laps from the end, when he collided with Skye Girard, a lapped rider he was trying to pass. The collision injured Tommy's hand and sent him tumbling through a gravel trap. Roger went on to finish third, but with the Supersport race still to run that afternoon, Tommy's points lead seemed to be in jeopardy.

Tommy headed to the on-site Salinas Valley Memorial Medical Center, where Dr. Art Ting told him that he'd broken a bone in his right hand, the hand that he needed to activate the front brake—extremely important, especially at a technical track like Laguna. Back in the pits, crew chief Joey Lombardo busied himself preparing Tommy's ZX-6R. "At that point, it was just, 'Whatever you want to do, Tom,' " Lombardo says. "The talk was that he might try to race, so I told my guys, 'Just make the thing easy to ride.' "

One of the Haydens' buddies had a bicycle sitting in the pit, and Lombardo noticed that it had thick handgrips. The crew cut the grip off and wired it onto the Kawasaki's throttle so that Tommy wouldn't have to make a tight fist. Tommy returned and announced that he would try to race, and Lombardo counseled him: "Just do the best you can, and try to score some points."

Roger was almost as adversely affected by the injury as Tommy. With doctors milling around the pits and a palpable tension in the team truck, it was hard to focus on his responsibilities. Riders are accustomed to blocking things out when they have to perform, but this was definitely a situation in which having your brother for a teammate was a negative. "That's an example of where things are *not* good," Fahie says. "Before Tommy fell down, everything was gravy. Tommy was on fire, and Rogie was feeding off that. When Tommy hucked it off into the weeds, things started going downhill, because all of a sudden Rog was worried."

Ironically, Nicky actually *benefited* from Tommy's crash. Obviously, he was concerned about his brother's welfare, but that worry was a welcome distraction. "I was so bummed, it

actually helped me before the race, to quit thinking about the start," Nicky says of Tommy's crash in *DTK*. "Before the race, I was actually quite relaxed."

Because Laguna's technical nature makes passing difficult, getting a good start is paramount. When the red light flashed off, Nicky came through, nabbing the holeshot and leading into tight turn 2. So strong was the getaway that Earl—watching on pit road—worried that perhaps Nicky had jumped the light, but all was well. When the pack came around to complete lap 1 of 32, Nicky had already established a gap on second-place Rossi, and he knew he was having a special day.

Nicky clicked off several laps at the front, and although he initially worried that perhaps the Italian was toying with him, he was able to respond to each of Rossi's attacks by lowering his own lap times. Meanwhile, Edwards was charging through the pack to third after getting hung up on the start, and on lap 16, he put a pass on Rossi at the top of the Corkscrew to steal second.

Although the stakes had Earl so stressed out that he could barely watch (instead, he simply stared at his clipboard, only glancing up whenever the stopwatch said his son was due), Nicky's race at the front was technically boring: He was on his own level, and no one could challenge him. Edwards tried making a late charge from second, but by then his tires were shot.

As he completed the final lap, Nicky found himself remembering the time eight years earlier, when he had earned the disapproval of Rob Muzzy by crashing during his first tryout, on that very same track. "I was definitely thinking about that story," Nicky says, "especially as I was coming into that last corner."

When Nicky crossed the finish line with a 1.941-second lead, a huge weight was removed from his shoulders. It had

BELOW: With Michael Jordan watching from the Red Bull Energy Center above turn one, Roger and Tommy grab the lead off the start in the Supersport race. The hillside and structure have since been removed to create more runoff room. (Riles/Nelson)

RIGHT: Tommy grabs a wheelie at Road Atlanta during the 2005 season. With confidence borne from his Supersport title, he is stronger than ever. (Riles/Nelson)

been three years since his last win, and it felt so good that he would later call it the happiest day of his life. He certainly made the most of it. During his cool-down lap, he stopped to pick up an American flag from a spectator and to do a smoking burnout in the Corkscrew. When he made it back to pit road, rather than pull into victory circle, he put Earl on the back of his RC211V and did another lap, in the dirt track tradition.

Earl was so overcome that he forgot to reprimand Nicky for breaking his "no showing off" rule. "I hate it when I watch an NFL game and see a guy do a dance when he gets a first down," Nicky says. "I think you should just do your job—act like you've been there before and like you'll be there again—but sometimes I see myself doing the same thing. I pretty well wear my heart on my sleeve, and I like to celebrate sometimes as well."

When he finally did make it to the victory podium, Nicky even did a Kentucky jig, just like he had after the Hayden sweep at the 2002 Springfield TT. It was the first time the American national anthem had been played at a Grand Prix since Kenny Roberts Jr.'s win in Motegi five years earlier, and the occasion was so emotional that it even swept up Nicky's competition, including Edwards, who had held off Rossi for the runner-up spot: "I didn't win my home Grand Prix, but I was happy for Nicky at the same time," the Texan said in Neale's documentary. "He has worked hard, and I've known Nicky since he was 8 years old. To be there and be a part of two Americans going 1-2 at the Grand Prix was a memorable experience, for sure."

"You just couldn't write a better breakthrough," says Kenny Roberts Sr., who never had the pleasure of winning a home Grand Prix, and who admitted that Nicky's win brought the hairs up on his neck.

"I was thinking about when I was a kid and what my mom and dad had done," Nicky said in the packed post-race press conference. "I can honestly remember going to Daytona one year to race amateurs, and our roof was leaking so bad that my dad put buckets under the roof. You may laugh and think it's funny, but the dude spent the money we needed on a roof to go racing—whatever it took."

While the celebrations were still happening, Roger helped Tommy get suited up for the Supersport race (just as Tommy had helped him after his bicycle injury earlier in the year). Some of the riders around Tommy on the grid had worried that the injured bone in his braking hand would prevent him from even making it through the first corners, but they needn't have worried: While Roger was barely bested by Jason DiSalvo at the finish, Tommy fought through the pain to finish sixth and retain a 41-point lead in the standings. "Tommy stepped up," Fahie says. "If you only knew how bad that really was . . . For him to even function—let alone ride—was an incredible feat."

Nicky's home MotoGP win changed his status, establishing him as a legitimate contender. Even while Rossi had ruled the past few seasons, the industry was looking for riders with the potential to be the next king. Suddenly, Nicky was one of those riders, and although his passport wouldn't help him with European sponsors, Dorna (the MotoGP promoter) was excited about his potential to help grow the sport in the United States "There's no question that that day changed things," says International Racers' Steven Dicterow. "All of a sudden, the phone was ringing off the hook. It really moved him into a whole new bracket." Three weeks after the Red Bull USGP, all three Hayden brothers made an appearance on the *Tonight Show* with Jay Leno.

The win also helped Nicky believe in himself. Although he crashed out of the next race, in England, he qualified on pole in Germany and finished third in the race. He ended the

year with four straight podium finishes, including runner-up results in Phillip Island (where he gave Rossi a run for his money) and Valencia. At season's end, he was third in points behind Rossi and Melandri, his best finish ever.

"There are different types of learning," Kenny Roberts Sr. explains. "Either you're really quick when you first get [into Grand Prix racing], and then you start falling off the thing, or sometimes you're a little bit slower and then work up to your peak. I think Nicky makes little steps, but they're always forward."

Back in the United States, Tommy finished the year by successfully defending his Supersport title, with Roger second on the season, 19 points back. "Looking back now, it would have been championships three years in a row without the penalty in 2003," Tommy says. "That would've been a pretty good string of titles."

Tommy had sat out the latter part of the Superstock series to focus on the 600s and allow his hand to heal, but Roger

scored his first 1000cc win, in the finale—an exciting race that saw him power around the outside of DiSalvo in Road Atlanta's treacherous final turn. "He has an attitude that's just like: 'I'm doing what it takes to go to the front,' " Fahie says of Roger. "He's got that focus and grit, and it's not something that everybody has."

The youngest Hayden brother's riding finally had people taking him seriously, and with his contract up and other teams showing interest, Roger told Kawasaki that to keep him, they'd have to reenter the Superbike class in 2006. Kawasaki didn't want to lose such a promising talent, so although they had been thinking of delaying the return until 2007, they changed their plans and agreed to enter both brothers in the premier class the following season.

Roger was also growing up in other areas. Earlier that year, he had finally moved out of the little room in his parents' house and into one of his investment apartments, and after the season was over, he purchased a house just down the street from Earl and Rose. "The neighbor told my parents he was thinking about selling his house, so we went up there and talked to him and walked through it," Roger says. "It worked out perfect. I can ride right out of my garage, or take a five-minute walk home for dinner. It's the best of both worlds."

In addition, the brothers had decided to sell their California condominium and upgrade to a nearby house. They stocked the large garage with motocross bikes, Supermoto machines, and road and mountain bicycles, and they filled the closets with clothes. "We set it up to where we could just show up with ourselves, and we'd have everything we needed," Tommy says. The Hayden boys were ready for a full-on assault on the 2006 season.

Holding a special award presented to him by his team, Tommy
Gun and his crew celebrate back-to-back Supersport titles at the
Road Atlanta finale in 2005. (Riles/Nelson)

RIGHT: Following a third-place finish behind Valentino Rossi and Loris Capirossi at the popular Italian Grand Prix, Nicky borrows an umbrella girl's wig on the podium. "With the atmosphere here and the crowd, these are the days you really enjoy," Nicky said. (Andrew Northcott)

BELOW: Riding on a subpar Laguna Seca track following a botched resurfacing job, Nicky heads down the Corkscrew toward the roughest section. His dirt track background made him relatively comfortable with the bumps. (Andrew Northcott)

CHAPTER 13 | CHASIN' A DREAM

Prior to the 2006 season, Nicky had figured he would be the clear number-one rider at Repsol Honda. After one acrimonious season with the squad, Max Biaggi had left the team and the series, and Honda had brought up Dani Pedrosa—Nicky's fourth different teammate in as many years—from the 250cc ranks. Just 20 years old, Pedrosa was a diminutive rookie, but he nonetheless came in with a lot of promise, having earned three world titles in the support ranks—more than even Valentino Rossi had done by that age. Pedrosa was heralded as a champion in the making, whereas Honda was asking Nicky (and not Pedrosa) to ride the 2006 Suzuka 8 Hours, a favor normally performed by premier-class rookies.

During pre-season testing, Nicky found himself developing two different bikes—the updated RC211V that was based on the 2005 model, and the all-new machine that most called the "Brno type" (because it had first been seen by the public at the previous year's post–Czech Grand Prix test), but which was officially called the "new generation" RCV. Meanwhile, Pedrosa and the satellite-team Honda riders all rode only the revised bike.

Because he was splitting his time between two machines, Nicky turned far more laps in testing than any other rider, his only break coming in the form of minimal tire-testing responsibilities from Michelin. Unfortunately, his lap times weren't particularly impressive—especially those posted on the new-generation bike—and a crash at Australia's Phillip Island damaged his confidence a bit. Although the engines were more powerful than ever, electronic rider aids were doing an even better job of controlling them, and Nicky's ability to slide a bike continued to lose its usefulness. His detractors had become more vocal, with the European press in particular saying that Nicky could only win at home, and that his rookie teammate would eclipse him immediately.

It wasn't the most auspicious of off-seasons, and Nicky was feeling the pressure as he worked out one day between tests in his local Owensboro gymnasium. The facility has a small chapel on the ground floor, and after his workout, Nicky decided to pay it a visit. "I went in there and said a prayer," he recalls. "I told myself that I can only control what I do—ride every lap my hardest, every session, every weekend, and don't take any shortcuts. After that, I kind of felt like we'd just see what happens."

On the positive side, Nicky was happier than ever with his immediate team. He and crew chief Pete Benson were completely in harmony, and he was also communicating well with his engine technician, Tetsuo Kinoe. Data technician Ramón Aurín was a particularly hard worker, and mechanics Mark Lloyd, Craig Burton, Koji Kaminakabeppu, and Jarmo Heljo were all performing well.

As the season approached, Nicky and his crew were leaning toward choosing the standard RC211V that the rest of the Honda riders would be using. It was more of a known quantity, and it gave Nicky better feel in the rear, but HRC had different ideas. MotoGP would be switching to an 800cc platform in 2007, and although Honda didn't admit it publicly, the smaller, new-generation bike—though still at a full 990cc—represented a sort of transition model that would help them gather data to prepare for the smaller-displacement machine that would replace it. Without Nicky riding that motorcycle, it would be difficult to gather information that would be meaningful beyond 2006.

As the lead rider, Nicky understood that he had a certain responsibility to perform this development work, but at the same time, he had his future to consider. He was in the last year of his contract, and he knew that his days at Honda would be over if he didn't have an exceptional season. The handicap of an unfinished bike was the last thing he needed.

Things went better at the official IRTA test in Barcelona. Colin Edwards posted the fastest time on the wet track, but Nicky—who had turned many laps in the rain over the winter—was right behind him with the second-quickest time.

With just one more test remaining before the season

opener, and with considerable pressure from Honda, Nicky decided to race the new-generation bike, in hopes that it would eventually become enough of a benefit to erase any early disadvantage. "There was no secret some of the big boys wanted to see that bike ridden," Nicky says, "and that was made pretty clear. With a contract about to be up at the end of the year, the last thing I could afford was bad results, but I needed the boys who sign the checks to be behind me."

Nicky started the season off well with four consecutive podium finishes, which made eight straight going back to the previous season. Meanwhile, Rossi was suffering some rare misfortune, getting knocked down at round one and encountering problems with chassis vibration and motorcycle reliability. The result was that after round three, Nicky was leading the points race.

Not that he wasn't having his own problems: A bout of bronchitis ended his podium streak in Le Mans and the new-generation RCV had such serious clutch issues that the bike would sometimes wheelie uncontrollably on starts.

The clutch abuse required for a good start developed excess heat that warped the plates, so pulling in the lever no longer completely disengaged the clutch. As a result, downshifts became quite harsh, creating problems entering corners. Nicky could prevent excess heat by babying the clutch on the start, but that slow start would allow the leaders to get away on the first lap, and because times were so close, catching them would be impossible.

Rossi started to turn his season around at Mugello, sending his home crowd into hysterics with a victory, and while Nicky rode to a third-place finish (and then celebrated by donning an umbrella girl's red wig on the podium), Capirossi's runner-up finish meant that he and Nicky were tied for the points lead, at 99. Unfortunately for Capirossi, a terrible, multirider crash on the start of the Catalan Grand

BELOW: In one of the strangest race finishes in recent memory, Nicky takes to the gravel trap beside Assen's final turn, moments before crossing the line with his second MotoGP win. The victory proved he could win outside the United States (Andrew Northcott)

LEFT: Nicky's "new generation" 2006 RC2IIV. Convinced by Honda to use the bike, Nicky and Benson struggled all season to find an ideal setup. (Honda)

Prix two weeks later put him out of the title race with a badly bruised chest. Nicky was by now using a 2005 clutch that was more reliable at the cost of some performance, and he was still unsatisfied with his bike's chassis. Nicky nonetheless managed a runner-up finish, and he was once again alone at the top of the points. Winner Rossi, however, was now third, 29 points back.

The slow progress with Nicky's RCV—caused in part by an industrial accident at the HRC factory that killed a worker and triggered extra safety measurements—was becoming frustrating. "I know HRC is working hard," Nicky said at the time, "but to be honest, we really aren't seeing as much stuff as we had thought."

Next up was Assen, Netherlands, where Nicky engaged in an epic fight at the front with Edwards, who led most of the race. Nicky got by toward the end, but Edwards re-passed him on the last lap and looked set to win. Going into the final chicane, Nicky made a move but hit neutral while trying to downshift to second, and he had to stand the bike up and head through the gravel trap. Fortunately for him, Edwards also made a miscue and went off track, then slid on a section of artificial grass and was thrown from his bike.

"I was bummed, because I thought, 'Man, I just blew it,' " Nicky says. "Then I saw him getting a handful in the Astroturf and getting sideways, and I thought, 'Oh, hold up—this one ain't over yet!' I kind of tucked back in and got to the finish line." It was the second premier-class win of Nicky's career and the 200th for Honda.

During a practice crash, Rossi had suffered broken bones in his right wrist and left foot, leading to a last-place grid spot after qualifying. Despite a heroic eighth-place result in the race, the champ was now 46 points down on Hayden, who led Pedrosa—second in the standings—by a whopping 42. By now, it was clear to even his detractors that Nicky really did

have a shot at the title, and—deciding that risking an injury at the Suzuka 8 Hours would be ill-advised—Honda took that assignment off his agenda.

A few days later, just across the English Channel at Great Britain's Donington Grand Prix, Nicky's fortunes took a turn for the worse. Given new parts to test in practice, he never had time to find the right setup, and after qualifying a lowly 11th, he overshot a corner during the race and was lucky to make seventh by the finish. Pedrosa and Rossi went 1-2, eating into the points lead, and Nicky's crew was gutted. "That's one thing I like about my team," Nicky says. "If we have a bad race, you can tell. It's not like they just shake it off and head to the bar. When you put that much effort into it, it's *supposed* to hurt."

There was mounting criticism that Nicky—whose lead had now shrunk to 26 points—was choking under the pressure, but he came through with a third-place finish in Germany's round 10 at the Sachsenring. It was a knock-down, drag-out fight among the top six for much of the race. Near the finish, Hayden had to hold off Pedrosa (whose front tire pushed his teammate hard enough to rub much of the Repsol logo off his leathers). Meanwhile, Rossi took the victory and moved to second in points, 26 behind the American.

On the day after the German Grand Prix, Nicky grabbed a flight to Los Angeles for a Dorna press conference in Hollywood and the premiere for *The Doctor, the Tornado & the Kentucky Kid*, the Ewan McGregor–narrated documentary that Mark Neale had shot at the previous year's Red Bull USGP. From there, Red Bull chartered Nicky a Wednesday flight north to Monterey, site of his debut MotoGP victory.

This time around, the scenario was markedly different coming into Mazda Raceway Laguna Seca. Nicky had been a bit of an underdog before, but he was now a MotoGP points

OPPOSITE TOP: Nicky debriefs with Pete Benson in the Repsol Honda garage during the 2006 season. Nicky credits the Kiwi crew chief with helping him reach the next level, just as Merlyn Plumlee did back in AMA Superbike. (Andrew Northcott)
OPPOSITE BOTTOM: Following Nicky's home win, his results took a downturn as he continued to struggle with setup. Here, he and Benson try to come to terms with the RC211V in the garage at the Czech Grand Prix. (Andrew Northcott)

leader who had won in the series' previous visit to the circuit. In addition, whereas Nicky had enjoyed a distinct home-court advantage in 2005, most of his competition was now at least somewhat familiar with the track. In addition, $7 million in additional safety-related changes had removed the Americans' secret lines, serving as somewhat of an equalizer.

Still, "level playing field" would not be an appropriate term: Despite a recent repaving, the circuit was so bumpy in spots that officials worried that it might not hold up through the weekend. A fluke heat wave had hit the area, making for hellish 102-degree temperatures that caused some spectators to pass out, and with record 147-degree ground temperatures exacerbating the track-surface problem, the decision was made to postpone all of Sunday's AMA activity until after the MotoGP race.

Whereas he had dominated the entire weekend at his first home-country Grand Prix, Nicky was working with an imperfect setup this time around. He barely made the second row in qualifying, but a blazing start in the race put him in third after the first lap. A strong pass on Kenny Roberts Jr. moved him to second about a third of the way through, and another move on Chris Vermeulen—who had started strong but was struck by fuel problems—got Nicky the lead. From there, Nicky never looked back, becoming the first rider to win a USGP from anywhere but the front row.

Meanwhile, Laguna blew a big hole in Rossi's title hopes, as the Italian only managed to qualify 10th, and after fighting his way up to 4th late in the race, his Yamaha YZR-M1 was hobbled first by a chunking tire and then by overheating problems. Rossi dropped out with just two laps remaining, leaving him fourth in points—51 in arrears of Hayden. Pedrosa—runner-up in his first visit to Laguna—was 34 points behind Nicky in second. Just six rounds remained.

Nicky's up-and-down pattern continued, as the USGP win was followed by some bad results at Brno in the Czech Republic and at Sepang in Malaysia, where Rossi's popularity among his peers was glaringly obvious. "I followed him out for the sighting lap at Malaysia," Nicky says, "and the whole paddock comes out to wish him good luck—all the 125 teams and everyone. I'm thinking, 'This is what I'm up against.'"

Nicky had tested a new chassis after Brno, and he'd chosen it for Sepang. It proved better in some areas but worse in others, and although he managed to finish fourth, Rossi's win and Pedrosa's third place—despite a gashed right knee suffered in practice—meant the margin narrowed to just 22.

At this stage, many were criticizing Nicky for riding somewhat defensively, but asking him to throw caution to the wind would be unrealistic. Yes, his advantage was being diminished, but the fact was that the tactical approach was paying dividends. Nicky had led the series ever since its third round, and he was the only rider to have scored points in every race. He knew very well that just a single crash could ruin his title hopes.

At no race was the importance of this balance between prudence and aggression more evident than at Phillip Island. Aware that a good finish was vital, Nicky qualified on pole for the first time all year, but as the riders lined up for the race, rain threatened on the horizon. For just the second time ever (the first had been at the previous season's Estoril Grand Prix in Portugal), officials announced that the new flag-to-flag regulation would be in effect. This meant that no red flag would be waved in the event that it did rain; instead, the race would remain live, although riders would be allowed to pit and change to a motorcycle fitted with rain tires if they so desired (none had done so in Estoril).

Nicky suffered a horrendous getaway, his uncooperative clutch slipping all the way to the first turn. Incredibly, after

After Honda motocrosser Ernesto Fonseca was paralyzed in a crash in March, Nicky wore his friend's No. 10 on his helmet throughout the 2006 season. (Hayden collection)

Rossi talks with his title rival during the pre-race press conference for the Australian Grand Prix. The race would include a controversial incident involving the two riders. (Andrew Northcott)

Phillip Island 2006

starting from pole, he was in 16th position at the completion of lap one. "I was feeling some heat there," he said after the race. "I saw Valentino and Pedrosa up there, and I knew I really had to recover."

Seven laps in, with Nicky only up to 10th, the rain came, and riders began pulling into the pits. Calling upon his Daytona 200 experience—and the fact that his was one of the only crews to have practiced for this situation during the pre-season—Hayden performed a flawless bike switch (though he very nearly sideswiped Capirossi on the exit), while other riders floundered in the unfamiliar scenario. Suddenly, Nicky found himself battling for position with Rossi.

The pair began carving their way through the pack, Nicky following in Rossi's wake, but on the 15th lap, controversy hit. A crash by Carlos Checa prompted a corner worker to wave a yellow flag, indicating that no overtaking was allowed, yet Rossi—who later said he hadn't seen the flag—passed Casey Stoner to gain a position. Knowing that such a move is supposed to result in a 10-second penalty, Nicky refrained from following Rossi by Stoner until the flags stopped waving; then he continued his race, confident that he would be scored as finishing ahead of the champ at the finish. Despite being temporarily held up, Nicky eventually worked his way up behind Rossi again, but Valentino nipped Sete Gibernau near the end to take third, with Hayden fifth.

As it turned out, the race direction officials had missed Rossi's illegal move, and although they later—after HRC's official protest—admitted that they had made a mistake, the regulations made no allowance for instituting a penalty after the race.

"We have a rule," Nicky said afterward. "It's on tape—it's plain as day that he passed under waving yellow. I'm a little bummed because if it was the other way around, I think I would have gotten penalized. But the truth is, Valentino beat me, and I've just got to keep rolling." HRC president Suguru Kanazawa publicly demanded that actions be taken, but the upshot of it all was that Rossi had gained valuable points and was just 21 behind Nicky.

Aware that Hayden's contract with Honda was up at season's end (and aware of his treatment by HRC over the course of the season), both Yamaha and Ducati had been in serious negotiations with Nicky's management since July's German Grand Prix. Both teams had presented offers that were significantly better than what Honda was offering. "Yamaha has often thought of [hiring] Nicky," said Yamaha team manager Davide Brivio, who had been involved in the company's initial try for Hayden, before his rookie season. "Personally, I consider him a great rider."

Repsol Honda eventually increased their offer (although it was still less than what Yamaha and Ducati were bidding), and on Friday at the following week's Japanese Grand Prix, they announced Hayden's re-signing, for two more years. Nicky has always been motivated much more by winning than money, and he suspected that Honda—who had had the best 990 when the four-stroke platform was adopted in 2002—might also have the top 800 in 2007. Although he was frustrated by some of HRC's actions, he was extremely pleased with his immediate crew and didn't want to lose that environment. In addition, he had gotten assurances from Honda bosses that he would have at least equal equipment to Pedrosa's in 2007.

The Motegi circuit is owned by Honda, and after the announcement, top officials from the company were on hand to see Nicky finish fifth, while Rossi slashed his deficit to just a dozen points with a runner-up finish to Capirossi. More important, Motegi saw Repsol Honda make a concentrated effort—both before and after the race—to rectify Hayden's never-ending clutch woes.

A standard, coil-spring clutch replaced the diaphragm-spring unit for the race, and although Nicky still pulled a wheelie off the start line, the clutch proved more durable. The next day, while Pedrosa tested Honda's new 800cc RC212V for the first time, Nicky and his crew tried a shortened clutch lever that cleared his outer fingers, enabling additional lever travel. It worked, and a special, dogleg lever was quickly prepared for Estoril. In addition, HRC came up with a system that limited revs off the start. The decreased wear and tear on the clutch more than made up for the lessened likelihood of a holeshot.

Only two rounds remained: Estoril and Valencia.

Meanwhile, Tommy and Roger were having a rougher go of it back in the States, during Kawasaki's reentry into the AMA Superbike class. Things had kicked off well enough, with Tommy managing a top-five finish in the premier class at Daytona, while Roger won the Supersport race. Saturday at Barber's round two went nicely as well, with Tommy picking up another top-five finish in Superbike and Roger becoming the Supersport title favorite with win number two. In Sunday's second half of the Superbike doubleheader, however, Roger was knocked down by lapper James Kerker, and he slid into a trackside wall and broke the tibia and fibula bones in his right leg. Shortly thereafter, Aaron Yates barged into Tommy on the last lap, knocking him from second to seventh.

Roger missed the next race at California Speedway, but although he opted to sit out much of the Superbike season during his recovery, he showed up with a broken leg at Infineon Raceway's round four to try and salvage some Supersport points. He qualified in 10th position, but the race was cancelled due to bad weather.

In June, Tommy crashed and slid into a wall during a test at Mid-Ohio, breaking his wrist and suffering a concussion. He recovered in time to garner a runner-up Superbike finish at Laguna Seca—his first Superbike podium ever—the day before Nicky won his second Red Bull USGP race. That would be the highlight of his year, and at season's end, Tommy ended up sixth in Superbike (for the third time in his career), while Roger was 17th in Superbike and fifth in Supersport.

Early in his Grand Prix career, Nicky had failed to obtain full enjoyment from his brothers' good results when he was struggling. Now that he was enjoying a strong season, the situation was exactly the opposite: After his strong runner-up finish to Rossi at Barcelona, Nicky watched the live timing from Miller Motorsports Park on the Internet in his hotel. Both of his brothers were riding injured, and although Tommy was fifth in Superbike and Roger second in Supersport, Nicky knew they had hoped for better from this season. "It kind of mellowed out my enjoyment of the day," Nicky says.

When the AMA season was over, Tommy's contract was up, and he decided to switch teams to Yoshimura Suzuki for 2007. The team had taken seven of the last eight AMA Superbike championships (Nicky's 2002 crown with Honda being the sole interruption), and although Tommy was disappointed to part ways with his immediate crew, he figured making the move would help his chances in the premier class.

"Toward the end of the summer, there were a lot of things that I felt could have been handled better," Tommy said. "I was kind of disappointed in how I was being treated, and I just decided that maybe it was time to make a change. Yosh has a great Superbike track record over the years, so hopefully I can go over there and continue with that."

In the meantime, though, Tommy had other things on his mind. Nicky had what could be the two most important races of his life coming up, and Tommy was headed to Europe to lend a hand as his big brother.

CHAPTER 14 ON TOP OF THE WORLD

ABOVE: Nicky during qualifying for Portugal's Estoril Grand Prix, where he put it on the front row. "Tomorrow's race is going to be a shootout," he said Saturday afternoon. "I think all the fans at home should get ready for it and take the phones off the hook, because it's going to be a good one." He had no idea. (Andrew Northcott)

With Nicky and Tommy still recovering from surgery, the Hayden brothers wait impatiently to ride their motocross bikes after the 2006 season. (Chris Jonnum)

Nicky breaks out the bubbly on the Valencia podium. (Andrew Northcott)

Nicky dropped to his knees outside turn six of Portugal's Autodrómo Fernanda Pires da Silva (Estoril) and pounded his right fist into the gravel three times, struggling to comprehend what had just happened. His helmet off, he got to his feet and marched away from the track, waving his left fist in the air and bellowing at the sky and at his teammate, Dani Pedrosa. Earl had taught his sons not to swear in public, but Nicky wasn't holding back this time. "That's bullshit!" he roared.

It was the second-to-last round of the 2006 MotoGP series, and Nicky had entered the race with a 12-point lead on Valentino Rossi in the title chase. Through a combination of consistent riding on his part and misfortune on that of the five-time premier-class champion, Nicky had a very real chance of wrapping up his first world title two weeks later at the final round in Valencia. All he had to do was get through Estoril with a decent finish. Unbelievably, however, just four laps into the race, Pedrosa lost control of his RC211V while pushing his front wheel under his teammate in the third-gear corner, trying to take over third place. Pedrosa fell off the low side and collided into Nicky. As the world television audience looked on disbelievingly, Hayden's handlebars were torn from his hands, and the two Repsol Hondas and their riders tumbled off the track and into the gravel.

"When I first got hit, it was so hard, I instantly thought it was over," Nicky says. "I was sliding across the ground, and I wasn't worried about whether I was hurt or that I wasn't going to win that race, or anything else. I remember just thinking, 'Well, there it goes. My title hopes just went down the drain with one race to go.' "

Nonetheless, Nicky had no sooner stopped tumbling than he was on his feet, sprinting to his downed bike and frantically motioning for corner workers to assist him in righting it. He was hoping that the damage would be minimal enough to allow him to reenter the race, but he soon realized it was futile, dropped the bike, and vented his frustrations. "It didn't even seem real—more like a dream," Nicky says. "I was just thinking, 'Is this really happening?' "

Considering the circumstances, many witnessing the scene were amazed that Nicky didn't physically attack the young Spaniard. "On that side of things, I'd like to think I'm pretty professional," Nicky explains. "As much as I wanted to pop him, I knew that definitely wasn't going to help me. The last thing I could afford at that point was a suspension from Valencia."

A good portion of Nicky's frustration was directed not at Pedrosa, but at HRC. Many had assumed that Dani would ride in support of Hayden, but just the previous week, HRC managing director Satoru Horiike had almost defiantly told reporters, "I have always said that Honda never, ever makes any team orders. If we make team orders, then this is not good for anyone—not for the fans, for the riders, for the mechanics, or anyone in the team. We will not do it."

Still, issuing explicit team orders (forbidding one rider to race his hardest, in order to help his teammate's points situation) is one thing, and simply explaining prudent tactics is another; Pedrosa was an inexperienced rookie, but no one had sat down with him before the race and described the gravity of the situation.

Nicky sat on the back of the team scooter, screaming his frustration into Tommy's back as his brother took the Estoril circuit's access road back to the paddock. Pedrosa's incredible mistake had left Nicky with zero points in the race; after having led the title chase for most of the year, his championship chances now seemed all but eliminated.

Bypassing the Repsol Honda garage ("It would have been easy to say or even do something I might regret," Nicky explains), the brothers headed straight to Nicky's motor home, followed shortly by Earl and Aldon. The mood was dark, and although the television was tuned to the race, they weren't paying much attention until someone noticed that Kenny Roberts Jr. and Toni Elias were giving Rossi a battle at the front. "I started screaming, pulling for somebody to beat him, just to give me a chance in Valencia," Nicky remembers.

Roberts led across the line to end the next-to-last lap, but—miscounting and momentarily thinking the race was over—he lost concentration and was passed by the other two riders. Rossi led into the last corner, but Elias pulled out of the champ's draft and nipped him at the line by just two-thousandths of a second to score the first premier-class victory of his career.

It wasn't much, but there in his motor home, Nicky suddenly felt a glimmer of optimism. "For whatever reason, that just gave me a sense of hope," he says. "It was almost like a sign, and it made me think, 'Hey, this one is far from over.'"

Had Rossi won, Nicky would have been down by thirteen points, but Elias's victory meant that he instead trailed by just eight. That meant that if Hayden could win at Valencia, he would only need one other rider to finish in front of Rossi in order to win the championship.

Would that rider be Pedrosa? The Spaniard visited Nicky in his motor home after the race, and—after quietly submitting to Nicky's heated expression of his displeasure—he promised that he would do everything he could to help at the finale. Shortly thereafter, while Earl went to Rossi's motor home to congratulate him ("I don't think many people would have done that," Rossi later said), Nicky met with a large group of journalists in the HRC hospitality center, expressing his dismay with the day's events. "I don't expect the guy to pull over and let me by, but I didn't expect *that*," Nicky said, his voice breaking. "I honestly would like to think . . . a guy with any kind of heart's got to know, with world championships, you don't get these opportunities all the time."

Honda had a test planned for Monday, and Nicky attended despite the fact that his right shoulder was quite sore following

LEFT: His AMA season having concluded one week earlier, Tommy came to Estoril to help with the final push for the MotoGP title. Nicky said his big brother's calm influence was invaluable. (Andrew Northcott) **BELOW:** Earl has some fun with the Beemer that Nicky won at Valencia for having the season's best total of qualifying times. The sports car escaped the fate of the 2nd Chance Auto lot, as Nicky sold it and gave the money to his crew. (Andrew Northcott)

Having switched to Yoshimura Suzuki over the off-season, Tommy races the potent GSX-R1000 superbike for the first time at Daytona in March 2007. (Riles/Nelson)

the crash. The proceedings were delayed by bad weather, so he and Tommy went for a run to stay loose, but when it became clear that nothing was going to be accomplished, they sped to the Lisbon airport just in time to catch an earlier flight home. It was time to circle the wagons and prepare for the Valencia finale two weeks hence.

Once back in the States from the Estoril debacle, Nicky went to the doctor for an MRI, which revealed that he had aggravated the same collarbone he had broken in a Supermoto crash two seasons earlier. The shoulder was quite sore, but Nicky had therapy done on it and trained as well as he could: "I tried to prepare for the last dance just like any other week— sticking to my routine."

Any plans Nicky may have entertained of keeping his injury a secret from Rossi pretty much went out the window on his flight from Madrid to Valencia. When Nicky took his seat on the plane, he found that his neighbor was one of Rossi's mechanics, who Nicky knew from when the technician used to work at Repsol Honda. The shoulder hadn't progressed much in the two weeks since Estoril, and Nicky still couldn't raise his arm above his head (surgery a month later would reveal that the plate on his clavicle had been bent and the bone re-broken). When the flight attendant asked him to store his carry-on bag in the overhead bin, Nicky tried ignoring the request, but after the second *por favor*, he had to ask her for some help. "Maybe [the mechanic] thought I was just trying to make conversation with a *señorita*," Nicky says, "but since she had a hard time fitting down the aisle, I doubt that. I guess he may have thought I'd just pushed myself too hard with Aldon's strength program, but I'm pretty sure he knew something was up."

Eight points doesn't sound like a huge deficit, but any shortfall to Rossi is daunting. The champ had won twice at the Circuito de la Comunitat Valenciana Ricardo Tormo and had made the podium in each of his last four outings—despite having started from the 15th spot on the grid in 2005! He had only failed to finish one premier-class race at the track (in 2000, his rookie year), and he had started from pole once, in 2003. Meanwhile, Nicky had raced three times at Valencia, and had scored a 16th in 2003, crashed out in 2004, and notched a third place in 2005.

That said, Valencia isn't one of Rossi's favorite circuits, and Nicky was a much stronger rider than he had been during the series' last visit to the track, whose tight, technical, counterclockwise layout suited his style quite well.

Following the events at Estoril, it hadn't taken long for video of both the crash and Nicky's poignant press conference to be posted on the Internet. The combination of the situation's injustice and Nicky's openness afterward had even fans who had previously criticized him coming to his defense, especially after postrace quotes from Pedrosa's mentor, Alberto Puig, were published. "Dani had a mathematical chance, so who would obligate him not to race?" Puig was quoted as saying. "A big deal is being made because this involves the leader of the championship and his teammate. The first thing Hayden had to do was get in front, which he hasn't done all year. I know it's terrible for Honda and for Nicky, but it could have happened to anyone."

Racing websites and magazines circulated editorials supporting Nicky and criticizing Pedrosa, Puig, and HRC, and racing fans the world over rallied to Nicky's defense. Even Rossi weighed in, according to a quote from the Spanish press: "There are two riders in Honda," he said. "One is a little rooster who is fifth in the world championship, and the other is a leader who's all alone."

Nicky would have plenty of support at Valencia as well. A strong contingent of Americans would be among the 129,446-strong crowd, including Michael Jordan, Kevin Schwantz, and

Ernesto Fonseca—the Honda motocrosser with whom Nicky had been hanging out at the 2002 Chicago trade show, where he had learned he would ride for Repsol Honda. The previous March, Fonseca had been paralyzed in a practice crash at his private track in Southern California, and Nicky had worn the Costa Rican's No. 10 on the back of his Arai helmet in tribute ever since.

Most important, the entire Hayden family—with the exception of Kathleen, who had responsibilities back at the University of Kentucky—would be at the race, and Tommy would once again be watching over his younger brother for the weekend. Aldon was on hand as well, as was Nicky's friend Seth Lawson. There would even be a film crew from MTV on hand to document Nicky's every move, as they gathered footage for a reality show—a distraction that Nicky deemed to be worthwhile. "I wasn't sure I wanted to take it on, because it does require a bit of time," he says. "But I was talking with my dad about what it could do for the sport in America, and I think I owe it to the sport to do it."

Upon his arrival in Valencia on Wednesday, Nicky spoke with Repsol Honda manager Makoto Tanaka to see what the team's plans were. Amazingly, it seemed that not only would there again be no team orders, but little would be done to try and smooth out what was obviously a very tense and awkward team situation. "I don't really agree with how it was all handled," Nicky says. "I don't sign anybody's checks, but we should have sat down and talked about giving each other room and trying to help each other—being real teammates."

After three decent practice sessions, Nicky posted the fifth-fastest time in qualifying, earning a second-row start, while Rossi took pole position. It was easily good enough for Nicky to wrap up the BMW M Award for the season's best accumulated qualifying times, with nearly seven seconds to spare over Edwards. (Later that weekend, he would give

Jordan a ride in his new sports car, but not before Earl had adorned it with one of his 2nd Chance Auto paper license plates; after the race, Nicky presented the car to his crew, who sold it and divided the money.) For the race, though, Nicky would have his hands full.

On Saturday night, Benson and Nicky sat down with Puig and Pedrosa (who had qualified one spot behind Nicky) for a serious talk. Dani confirmed that he would do anything he could to atone for his mistake. "It wasn't exactly like team orders," Nicky says. "It was just a gentlemen's agreement... The main thing is that we wouldn't be racing each other, because we were starting fifth and sixth. I told him that if he helped me, I wouldn't forget him."

For the most part, though, strategy was out the window, something that Nicky actually found refreshing. For most of the season, he had eschewed risk-taking as he carefully guarded a points lead; now, he could race flat out, without being conservative.

When the lights flashed off, Nicky got a good launch, but he had to brake when a bad-starting Rossi drifted across his path. Troy Bayliss—fresh off earning the World Superbike crown and substituting at Ducati Marlboro for an injured Gibernau—led into turn one, followed by teammate Capirossi, Pedrosa, and Stoner, with Nicky and Rossi nearly side-by-side in fifth. Nicky immediately took over the position and then quickly moved by Stoner for fourth. "I wanted [Rossi] to see how I was feeling and what I was prepared to do," Nicky says. "I wanted him to see me go through them."

While Rossi dropped back a spot to seventh, Nicky cut inside Capirossi to take over third on lap two. Pedrosa had taken over second, but he moved wide to let his teammate through on lap three. That put Nicky in second, and he set about catching the fleeing Troy Bayliss, reveling in the chance to throw caution to the wind.

ABOVE: An overcome Nicky stops and falls to his knees midway through his victory lap. In a true "Dewey Defeats Truman" moment, the pyrotechnic display prepared by the Valencia organizers emitted Rossi-yellow smoke. (Martin Heath) **RIGHT:** Earl gives Nicky his first hug as world champion in the Valencia winner's circle. It was America's first Grand Prix title since 2000. (Andrew Northcott)

ABOVE: At the second MotoGP round of 2007 in Jerez, an MTV camera crew films Nicky for a new series with the champion on the popular network. (Andrew Northcott)

RIGHT: Michael Jordan shakes Nicky's hand in Spain. The NBA legend owns a Suzuki satellite team on the AMA circuit, and he has attended the Valencia Grand Prix since 2004. (Andrew Northcott)

With three Honda riders between him and Nicky, who had by now closed up to the leader's rear tire, Rossi must have known he had to start a charge of his own, but on lap 5 of 30, the impossible happened: The champ's front tire lost traction in a slow left-hand corner and he went sliding off the track. Before the race, many had predicted that Nicky would fold under the considerable pressure at the last round, but no one thought that the normally imperturbable Rossi would make such a mistake.

Rossi remounted in last, and as the leaders came down the front straight to begin lap six, Nicky got the "ROSSI P20" signal on his signboard. Realizing that outright aggression was no longer advisable, Hayden immediately backed off a couple of percent and went into protection mode once again. "I definitely had to take some breaths for a few laps and kind of chill out," he says.

Capirossi soon began pressuring Nicky, who didn't put up much of a fight when the Italian came up on the inside on lap eight. Nicky began moving back up on Capirossi, but he knew that the slightest mistake at this point could be disastrous. "I felt pretty good," Nicky says, "but I was pushing right on the edge—as you would imagine, to be battling right at the front—and I thought, 'You know what? This is stupid. Let's just do what we have to do to get the heck out of here.'"

The second half of the race was interminable for Hayden fans, and Earl and Rose literally had their fingers crossed on pit row. However, there was a lot of real estate between Nicky and Rossi, along with no fewer than six Honda-powered riders (counting Roberts on the KR211V). "Maybe they knew it was for their best interests for the future," Nicky says. "For whatever reason, it seemed like these guys were all wanting to be team players."

With four laps to go, the words "ROSSI P13; P3 OK" were finally put on Nicky's signboard, indicating that third place was fine, but it wasn't until he followed Bayliss and Capirossi down the front straight for the last time that Nicky would let himself believe that the title was his. "When I came out of that last corner, the first thing I did was look for my team, hoping they were hanging over that wall," Nicky says.

Finally able to let down his guard, Nicky was overcome by emotions as he slowly circulated the track on his cool-down lap. Pedrosa—having dutifully followed his teammate home in fourth—came by to shake his hand, and Nicky patted the Spaniard on the head in recognition of his contribution. "It's hard to think that we'll ever completely put it behind us," Nicky said, "but I told him we'll be straight, and I've got to stay true to my word."

As for Rossi, it was the first time in five years that he had lost a world championship, and the fans seemed unable to grasp the day's developments (they weren't helped by the fact that Valencia's traditional season-end celebratory pyrotechnics featured the Doctor's signature yellow smoke). Rossi, however, retained his poise through his disappointment, riding up alongside Nicky and grabbing his arm in congratulations. "I saw that he cried on the victory lap, and that was nice," Rossi told the Italian press afterward. "I think that if I

LEFT: Still struggling to comprehend the day's events, Nicky sheds a tear in the emotional postrace press conference at Valencia. Those on hand gave him a standing ovation. (Andrew Northcott) OPPOSITE: In his first day aboard Honda's 2007 RC212V 800, during a postrace test at Valencia, Nicky takes his new No. 1 plate for a ride. "It was kind of Rossi's thing to keep his No. 46, and that's cool," Nicky said, "but where I come from, you definitely have to rock that No. 1 plate." (Andrew Northcott)

won, he'd have been 'happy' for me, and I'm happy for him. If someone else had to win, Nicky was at the top of my personal list. It was a great fight to the last race, but we were able to maintain the same relationship that we had in 2003."

"Rossi wins with class and he loses with class," Nicky said. "That's why you see the fans supporting him. He's done a lot for the series and for our sport. I need to remember that and try to do the same."

Upon finally making it to the winner's circle, Nicky located Earl in the throng and gave him a big hug. "You can tell them now," Nicky said in his father's ear, "whatever happens from here on out, Earl's Racing Team is officially a dynasty."

Meanwhile, it was early morning back in Kentucky, and Kathleen—having forgotten to set her alarm—was frantic to learn the results. "When I woke up, I went to look on the computer," she says. "The first thing I saw was that Rossi crashed, and then my computer stopped working! I was going nuts, and my roommates thought something bad had happened in Lexington. Finally I got through to my family, and I got to talk to Nicky on the phone for a split second. I wish I was there; that was hard."

Back in Spain, Nicky was ecstatic with having finally achieved his dream. "I always believed I would be world champion," Nicky says. "Even when I was 10 years old, I always believed—I swear, I believe this is the one thing I was put here to do."

The next few weeks were a whirlwind of activity. The day after his brother wrapped up the world championship, Roger got a surprise opportunity to try out Kawasaki's MotoGP machine during a journalist test at Valencia. Two days later, Nicky finally got his first ride on HRC's 800cc RC212V, which he found quite different from his championship-winning bike. "I've got some work to do," Nicky admitted. "It's not going to

be a real easy transition for me, but I feel confident that if I take some time, I'll be comfortable on that little thing."

That test was also Nicky's first chance to run the No. 1 plate since 2000, when he had defended his AMA Supersport crown (because he had moved to MotoGP after his Superbike title, he never wore the No. 1 in that class).

When Nicky finally got back home, Rose rented a large hall in Owensboro, hired a DJ, and invited family and friends for a victory party. Other than some wild dancing, things stayed fairly calm, although Eric Reynolds did hold Nicky to his promise that he'd drink a beer after winning the world championship.

A week and a half later was a rare combination MotoGP-AMA test in Malaysia, where Tommy was trying out his new Yoshimura Suzuki GSX-R1000 superbike and Nicky was back on the Honda RC212V 800. Unfortunately, Tommy would take a hard tumble, and following a rough ambulance ride, he was diagnosed with a concussion, a fractured ankle, and a broken scaphoid bone in his wrist. Back in the States, both brothers visited Dr. Art Ting in California to have corrective surgery performed on their injuries (Nicky's shoulder and Tommy's wrist).

As a result of their surgeries, there was a little less activity than normal at Sunset Downs over the early part of the winter, but the Hayden brothers did manage to do plenty of training. On New Year's Day, all three hopped on a plane to California to kick off their traditional off-season boot camp, and after a short winter testing break, they were back on tracks around the country and world, preparing for the 2007 season.

"I feel like the best is yet to come," Nicky says. "I truly believe that, and I'm definitely plenty motivated. I know one world championship's great, but you start adding to that with multiple world championships, and boy, you go into a whole new level."

Acknowledgments

I would like to thank the following people for their help in making this book possible:

• The Hayden family, for having faith in me, for being so generous with their time, and especially for generating and sharing so many great stories

• International Racers, for remembering they had been pitched on a Hayden biography, for knowing when the moment was right to start the project, and for taking a chance on this first-time author

• Davey Coombs and my other colleagues at *Road Racer X*, for agreeing to my taking on this project and for picking up the slack when it dominated my time

• My editor and publisher, David Bull, of David Bull Publishing, for his infinite patience and invariably helpful suggestions and advice

• All of the photographers whose work so beautifully complements my words

• Tom Morgan and Lucian Burg at Blue Design, for making such a handsome book

• The many people who, when told what I was working on, unhesitatingly agreed to being interviewed and who shared even more stories

• And most of all, my wife, Viviana, for her tremendous support when I hit rough patches, and for being patient when limited time prevented me from giving her the attention she deserved.